critical rationalism
and planning
methodology

Research in Planning and Design

p **Pion Limited, 207 Brondesbury Park, London NW2 5JN**

critical rationalism and planning methodology

A Faludi

p **Pion Limited, 207 Brondesbury Park, London NW2 5JN**

© 1986 Pion Limited

ISBN 085086 117 9

Printed in Great Britain by Page Bros (Norwich) Limited

Preface

The planning literature pays more and more regard to philosophy. Two books, *Planning Theory and Philosophy* by Mario Camhis (1979) and *Theories for Planning* by Sean McConnell (1981), bear evidence of this, as does a major article, "Planning theory and the philosophy of planning" by Nigel Taylor (1980). All give prominence to Popperian philosophy, and the earlier planning literature, although less explicitly concerned with philosophical issues, also shows attempts to apply Popper's work.

I concur with this trend, my concurrence being based on the argument (developed more fully in chapter 1) that (a) what goes under the flag of planning theory can be more properly described as planning methodology on *a par* with the methodology of science; (b) planning methodology must incorporate what is relevant in philosophy in general and in the methodology of science in particular. In so doing, naturally, planning methodology must also build on a proper understanding of planning issues. Unfortunately, the works quoted above partly misconstrue the task of planning methodology and/or misrepresent Popperian philosophy.

Clearly, we must study *various* philosophical schools and assess their relevance for planning methodology. This work singles out but one of them: the critical rationalism of Sir Karl Popper. I shall not examine the merits of Popper's methodology of the empirical sciences, but take his work as read. Nor shall I deal with the secondary literature, but limit myself to the implications of Popper's work as such. Furthermore, I shall aim for comprehensive coverage only of those parts which are relevant for planning. This includes parts of Popper's social philosophy, as well as of his methodology of science.

My conclusion will be that a planning methodology along the lines of Karl Popper is conceivable. But he does not offer it ready-made. 'Piecemeal social engineering', though often referred to, does not provide sufficient guidance for planning. So, a Popperian planning methodology needs to be reconstructed with building blocks culled from his work. This is what I shall do in this book. That methodology will be shown to be compatible with the approach proposed by myself in *Planning Theory* (1984, first published, 1973).

Throughout the text, I shall want to touch occasionally upon the debate concerning the proper scope of planning theoretical argument (see especially chapters 2 and 11). But it is not part of the purpose of this work to contribute towards the paradigmatic debate in planning theory, or in the broader field of policy science, operational research, and systems analysis for that matter. Nevertheless, the reader might expect a statement of my current position.

Planning Theory is firmly located in the tradition of what is commonly called procedural, as against substantive, planning theory (see chapter 1). As the name suggests, it is concerned with the procedures of planning, and also with its organisational forms.

Throughout the text of this work, I have attempted to relate it to my previous contributions on procedural planning theory. In assessing their nature, it is as well to realise what the issue was to which the distinction between procedural and substantive theory was a response: namely the disjointed nature of what went under 'planning theory' in planning curricula. It seemed quite innocent to suggest that some of this hotch-potch related to the subject-matter of planning and some to its organisation and procedures.

More controversial was the argument that procedures follow similar patterns, irrespective of the particular issues at stake, whereas substantive knowledge always remains contingent upon the nature of the problem, making it difficult to conceive of any general theory of planning oriented towards its substance.

Worse still was to come. Proceduralists intimated that their theory was applicable to a much broader field than just environmental planning. Having drawn inspiration from systems analysis, operational research, and cybernetics, they advocated that environmental planning should be viewed as but one out of a range of policy fields in which to apply the planning method. Therefore, they urged planners to leave their turf and let environmental planning amalgamate with management and policy planning generally.

The discussion related to central concerns of professional identity: which problems to focus on, and where to draw boundaries. It has been overtaken by another, more academic discussion since. Although sometimes conducted in the same terms of procedure *versus* substance, it is altogether different.

Its background was the prominence of radical social theory in the nineteen-sixties and seventies. Its adherents were suspicious of general approaches to decisionmaking and planning. Naturally, procedural planning theory, with its leanings towards such *technocratic* things as systems analysis etc was beyond the pale. Also, their main interest was not the conduct of planning and how to improve upon it. To them environmental planning—as indeed all interventions by public authorities—conformed to a pattern which, they claimed, was shaped by the prevailing—late-capitalist—mode of production. The task of theorists was seen as the analysis of planning as a phenomenon, so as to contribute towards the understanding of the state of our society.

At times the ensuing debate was acrimonious. Recently, however, there has been an increasing willingness to listen to each other. There is recognition on the part of radical planning theorists that the outcomes of planning are not simply a reflection of the forces of production. To some extent at least, the outcomes are also influenced by the organisation and procedures of planning. By the same token, procedural planning theorists have become even more interested in the way in which the context of planning influences its conduct. (However, this relationship has formed part of the problem of procedural planning theory all along, ever since Friedmann introduced the notion of a 'decisionmaking' or 'planning' environment; see Friedmann, 1967.) In this way, a common ground may emerge between the two camps.

It would, however, be too optimistic to expect them to coalesce. When procedural planning theorists—or planning methodologists—take account of the historical and political context of planning, they do so with a view to its greater effectiveness, and treat its sociopolitical context more or less as a given entity. Where radical planning theorists take account of procedures, they do so with a view to understanding planning better. *Their* strategies for improving its conduct—if indeed they are interested in such improvements—are *political* strategies. They seek out the weak points in the system, the areas where coalitions with disadvantaged groups might be formed, where the contradictions of capitalism can be demonstrated, and in that way they try to bring about change.

One can be sympathetic to societal change, and yet maintain that it is a different issue from the logic underlying the procedures of planning. This is the position a critical rationalist would take. But radical critics are never satisfied with distinctions such as these. They always maintain that who is in control is an issue which must also concern the methodologist. Indeed, in the so-called positivistic dispute (Adorno et al, 1976, first published in German in 1969), the very distinction between methodology and substantive social theory has been questioned.

I have participated on various occasions in the discussions referred to above. In this present work, however, these issues are peripheral. The aim is for a more cogent formulation of the concerns of procedural planning theory, having regard to critical rationalism.

Nevertheless, after having reformulated procedural planning theory as a decision-centred view of planning (in chapter 2), it will be appropriate for the sake of clarity to locate it (yet again) *vis-à-vis* other approaches. Another occasion when I return to this debate is in the final chapter, where possible criticisms of my Popperian planning methodology are discussed. But my position remains the same: I see methodology as different from substantive theory (be it radical or otherwise).

That final chapter will show also that there is an analogous debate going on in ethical theory. Certain forms of ethical theory—deontology— may pose a more serious challenge to my critical-rationalist planning methodology than do those coming from the radical camp. Be this as it may, ethical theory becomes one of the foremost areas that need to be investigated next.

This is not the only reason why this work does not even pretend to give any definite formulations. It is a study of *one* school of thought only. But, I attempt to explore the potentials of this one for planning methodology exhaustively. I do so by asking constantly what Popper's philosophy has to say about the methodological problems of planning in practice. There is more in this philosophy than many would seem inclined to grant.

This work locates itself in the environmental planning literature. The references are mainly to the literature in this field, and I expect it to be read above all by those concerned with environmental planning, broadly conceived (which I use as an umbrella term for all kinds of planning relating to the environment—that is what is conventionally described as urban and regional planning—but also environmental conservation, etc). I am the first to admit that this is somewhat at odds with my position that procedural planning theory is of general applicability, irrespective of subject matter. In principle, procedural planning theory (or planning methodology, as I now prefer to describe it) applies wherever planning occurs. Also, obviously, the implications of critical rationalism for planning methodology reach beyond environmental planning.

But environmental planning is the field to which I relate most easily. Nonetheless I have no difficulty in treating it as just one example out of several, where the preparation of decisions requires us to enter into prior analysis and where we design frameworks for future action based on this analysis (which is how I see planning; see chapter 2). I think I can render loyal help to those with a practical concern for environmental planning, whilst pointing out at the same time that their problems form part of a broader class.

Also, environmental planning is a field full of suggestions for those interested in planning as such: it is one of the most highly institutionalised forms of planning, in Western societies anyway, and a stamping ground for social reformers and experts of various kinds. It is more variegated—and perhaps more chaotic—than other fields of planning, but it is all the more interesting because of that.

Even as far as previous efforts to analyse the implications of critical rationalism for planning methodology are concerned, the environmental planning literature referred to in chapter 3 seems more extensive than any in other fields. A literature search conducted outside this field has revealed less than a dozen papers vaguely concerned with aspects of planning (Gendin, 1969; Shaw, 1971; Suchting, 1971; Freeman, 1975; Passmore, 1975; Gray, 1976; Mussachia, 1977; Urbach, 1978; Frazer and Boland, 1983). Most of these challenge Popper's condemnation of historicism. A systematic perusal of doctoral theses in the English language has revealed that none has been written on this topic.

The situation in Germany is clearly different and would warrant a separate study (see chapter 11). Even there, major works such as Spreer (1974), on the theory of economic planning, and Moewes (1980) on environmental planning, offer no more than restatements of well-known Popperian arguments about the nature of knowledge, about prediction, etc.

They do not depart from the problem of *planning* methodology (as against the methodology of the empirical sciences), let alone try to give an original Popperian solution.

On a more technical point, where multiple editions of a work exist, reference has been made to the edition actually used *and* to the original edition the first time it is mentioned. The same form is used whenever it seems important to draw attention to the time frame in which a work was written. All other references are solely to the edition which has been consulted by myself.

Nothing else remains to be said except to express the hope that this work will meet with criticisms as lively as those of *Planning Theory*. Without doubt, we planning academics need to intensify our efforts to clarify the methodology of planning in the face of its current crisis, which results from the widespread disenchantment with the role of government generally, and of analysis in policymaking in particular. What we can, and must, contribute is a clear view on what planning can—and *cannot*—achieve. Popper's critical attitude sets an excellent example.

A Faludi
University of Amsterdam
April, 1985

Acknowledgements

A few words seem apposite on the history of this work, the influences that I have undergone, and the help and encouragement given me by others.

I have experienced as particularly challenging criticisms by Eric Reade that my *Planning Theory* runs foul of the methodology of Karl Popper. They were paralleled by similar criticisms during internal discussions whilst still at Delft University of Technology. I decided to devote my inaugural lecture at the University of Amsterdam in 1978 to Popper, and argued that rationality as conceived in *Planning Theory*, should be seen as a methodological rule on *a par* with Popper's falsification principle. With important modifications, this is still the core of the argument of this book, set out in chapters 1 and 6.

I developed it further in a paper given at one of the Planning Theory Workshops of the *Education for Planning Association* organised by Eric Reade at the University of Manchester in 1981. In that paper, I also criticised other authors similarly concerned with the implications of Popper's teaching for our field, and this forms the subject of chapter 3. This paper was later published in modified form in *Urban Studies* (see Faludi, 1983). My contribution to the volume edited by Alan Hooper and Michael Breheny (1985), *Rationality in Planning*, also builds on this inaugural lecture. The consequentialist ethical theory of Popper and myself (see chapters 6, 7, and 11) was identified as such for the first time in that paper.

The influence on my work emanating from what I describe as the 'IOR-School' (see Faludi and Mastop, 1982), that is the work of the Institute for Operational Research (now the Centre for Operational and Organisational Research), should be evident throughout this book. I hope that the synthesis between their views and mine (see chapters 2 and 10) will eventually form the topic of another volume.

There is only one person whom I have asked to read and comment upon the manuscript besides the Editor (on whose role more below)— Dr Barrie Needham, whose work I quote (and mildly criticise) in chapter 3. In no way could I hope to have met all his criticisms in this final version. Many of them related to my decision-centred view of planning rather than my interpretation of Popper. They will have to wait until that forms the topic of the separate publication. But I can put on record my gratitude to Barrie Needham for having pointed out a major shortcoming in my interpretation of the implications of Popperian critical rationalism for planning methodology. As indicated, I had argued previously that rationality was on *a par* with falsification. Needham pointed out that it cannot be, because to Popper falsifiability is a demarcation criterion for distinguishing scientific statements from others. Rationality does no such thing. Rather, it helps in deciding what to do.

Our discussions on this point, all too short as they were, did not resolve the question of a demarcation criterion analogous to falsifiability for decisions. It only occurred to me later that what I had identified as

Popper's consequentialism was what we had been seeking. In this view I was encouraged by work done concurrently by Hans Mastop (in Dutch) suggesting that 'effectiveness' was the regulative idea with respect to decisions, analogous to truth for science (to be discussed in chapters 4 and 6). This is an interesting conjecture, but not wholly satisfactory. I cannot see effectiveness as the ultimate good towards which decision-making strives. But, the attention to effectiveness, to the consequences of action, is what to my mind distinguishes responsible decisionmaking. This confirmed me in my view of consequentialism as the Popperian demarcation criterion for decisions.

Of course, the reader will be able to appreciate these points much better after reading this work. Here, my purpose is merely to acknowledge my indebtedness.

To the Editor of the *Research in Planning and Design* series, Professor Allen J Scott, I owe my special thanks for the impressive care with which he has handled this book. He has always been extremely successful in not allowing our disagreements on matters of substance to interfere with his editorial judgement. I have profited a great deal from his thorough—and often quite detailed—comments. This book has become much better for the attention which he has given to it. His well-known predilection for historic – materialist—instead of critical rationalist—analysis means that, at the same time, he can in no way be held responsible for its failings.

It is customary also to thank secretaries for their meticulous work in turning illegible manuscripts into flawless copies which are the delight of any publisher. Early drafts of this work have indeed been in the tender care of various secretaries at the Institute for Planning and Demography of the University of Amsterdam where I teach, and for that I wish to record my thanks. Since then, technological innovation has hit, allowing me to produce the final draft on my word processor. My wife—being the only one at present to share this experience with me—has rendered inestimable assistance in transferring the first version onto disks so that I could make the endless revisions and additions which this medium allows. She has also given a helping hand with the bibliography, though her greatest help has been, as always, her cheerful and supportive sharing of my life.

To
Raya and Marion

Contents

Part 1

The problem of planning methodology

This part sets the scene. The aim is to arrive at a proper view of the problem which planning methodology should address. To this end, the discussion concerns the nature of methodology and of planning.

Since the topic of this book is *Popperian* planning methodology, I attend to Popper's own views of methodology as a theory of method in chapter 1. The same chapter shows that my views on normative planning theory expressed in my previous work, are remarkably similar—as are the mainsprings of our philosophies.

Chapter 2 introduces my current—decision-centred—view of planning as it has developed out of my previous work. In it, rationality figures as a decision rule. A key-concept is that of the definition of the decision situation, which I need in analysing the implications of Popperian philosophy in Part 2.

In chapter 3 I shall show why it is necessary to discuss the problem of planning methodology before attending to the implications of Popper's work. The reason is that the reception of his work in the planning literature reflects an inadequate understanding of this problem. In particular, some authors quoted misapply Popper's best known doctrine—that one should seek to falsify hypotheses—unthinkingly to plans. The mistake here is one of misconstruing the nature of plans. They are not hypotheses. A plan is a decision, albeit one of a special kind.

Still, the analysis of the reception of Popper in the planning literature, in chapter 3, will provide a good entry point for discussing the main topic of this book in Part 2: the importance of his critical rationalism to planning methodology.

From *Planning Theory* to planning methodology

Environmental planning now boasts an extensive theoretical literature. In my previous work (Faludi, 1973; 1984) the emphasis is on procedural planning theory. Since then, I have come to view my problem as methodological. The purpose of this book, as stated in the preface, is to develop a planning methodology in the spirit of the critical rationalism of Sir Karl Popper.

This chapter shows that this step towards planning methodology is a natural one. It also clarifies what to expect of planning methodology. I begin with distinguishing procedural from substantive, as well as positive (or empirical) from normative planning theory, both of which concentrate on rationality in planning.

Ten years after my proposing how to develop empirical planning theory of the procedural type, still no such theory has gained common acceptance. This warrants scepticism concerning the strategy proposed for developing it. In my empirical research since, 'methodological reflection'—the reconstruction of what decisionmakers and their planning advisers do in practice in the light of some norm of reasonableness—comes to the fore as an alternative.

Critics challenge me for clinging to rationality even though planning practice is far from rational. But whether it is borne out by practice is irrelevant to its validity. 'Rationality' is not like a hypothesis. By showing how decisions should be critically assessed, it answers to Popper's view of a methodological rule. As we shall see, its philosophical roots can be found in a secular view of humans as the makers of themselves, similar also to Popper's.

Based on this view of planning methodology and of the role of rationality, the chapter ends with the plan of this book.

1.1 Procedural planning theory

Knowledge is not sufficient for making plans. Rather, it must be applied to some purpose, and there must be organisations and procedures for coordination and implementation. This leads to the distinction between theory *in* planning (*substantive* theory) and theory *of* planning (*procedural* planning theory). My work relates to the latter.

Next to the procedural–substantive distinction, I make one between *positive* and *normative* theories of planning:

"... normative theory is concerned with how planners ought to proceed rationally. Behavioural approaches focus more on the limitations which they are up against in trying to fulfil their programme of rational action." (Faludi, 1973, page 4)

This distinction is not rigid. Improvements to planning must be based on knowledge of practice. Indeed, research is often guided by the desire to improve practice. Empirical planning theory—as I now prefer to describe positive theory—seeks knowledge about the organisation and procedures of planning but, in so doing, it usually aims at improving practice.

Empirical theories are sets of propositions concerning universal properties of reality. In explaining phenomena, we invoke theories—or laws—by demonstrating that the phenomena can be *deduced* from them. This is the *covering law model* of explanation. Thus, if a plan refrains from any but the most urgent pronouncements, leaving scope for future adjustments based on the awareness of uncertainties, then this is explained by invoking (1) the 'law' that uncertainty always leads to this form of 'process planning'; and (2) a reference to the existing situation as being one of uncertainty (the so-called initial conditions).

This is no more than an example. I do not claim that this law has been empirically validated. Indeed, *no* planning theory of this kind exists. True, the number of empirical studies grows almost by the day, but their results are difficult to compare. This problem is greater still in cross-national research where the need for a framework and for hypotheses becomes particularly evident.

Empirical theory formation, following the canon of scientific method, begins by exposing the rationale of the theory in question, including any normative assumptions underlying it. In the case of planning theory, I see this view of planning as one of rational decisionmaking leading to learning and ultimately to human growth. Based on it, a model of the object of research needs to be developed. In my case, this is a model of planning agencies which is based on an analogy with the human mind. Then, hypotheses must be derived from this model.

In speaking about 'testing' such hypotheses, and not about falsification, I have not been explicitly Popperian in the past. But this does not necessarily mean that I am 'positivistic', as both Taylor (1980) and to some extent Hooper (1982) think. There is no suggestion involved of generalising in an inductive manner from sense perceptions. Such misunderstandings must be partly due to my describing the outcome of this strategy as a 'positive' theory—which is the reason for changing this designation into 'empirical'.

This strategy has its labour-intensiveness in common with proposals by others. Up until now, still no such theory exists. This is quite apart from the dispute concerning the applicability of this strategy of empirical theory formation in the social sciences. If I am sceptical, then it is for pragmatic reasons.

1.2 Empirical planning theory: a digression?

Ever since discussing strategies for its formation, I am somewhat sceptical about empirical theory of the type described (see Faludi, 1973, pages 5 and 318). Also, I see a model of explanation which does not necessarily require fully-fledged empirical theories. In agreement with Kaplan (1964, pages 332–334), I distinguish between the pattern and the deductive model of explanation (Faludi, 1984, pages 22–24). In his otherwise very thoughtful review, Hooper (1982, page 245) misinterprets the reasoning behind this distinction. The deductive model relates to the standard model of scientific theory formation explained above, in that it requires the theoretical propositions so derived in explaining events as what one should rationally expect. The pattern model offers no more than a number of interlinking concepts reflecting assumed relationships in reality. It can be followed in lieu of the deductive model in cases where no theoretical propositions are available. Phenomena are 'explained' by fitting them into the model. Conceptual frameworks provide no more than this weak form of explanation. Now, although such a framework

"... is less reliable as a basis for action than more respectable theories are, it is more readily available to the point where it provides the *only* guidance. But to underline the difference from an empirically established type of theory still further, and to signify my awareness of the extent to which it is a theory influenced by my own values, I describe it as a *normative theory of planning*." (Faludi, 1984, page 29)

Unlike Hooper suggests, I do not try to reintroduce values "... apparently defined-out in the context of 'deductive models'". In my view, *all* theories incorporate values anyway. The strategy described above shows theory formation even to depart from values embodied in the rationale of planning. My point is merely that not all useful theories offer explanations of the deductive type. Unlike, for instance Reade (1976, page 95) arguing that a theory "... is taken to consist of explanations of causal relationships" and rejecting all other forms as not deserving that designation, I draw attention to another—more readily available—form of explanation.

Empirical research, on which I shall report in chapter 2, has since thrown further light on this matter. It concerned a comparison of Dutch and English local planning. Its dual aim was (a) to develop empirical planning theory, and (b) to make recommendations for practice. Preliminary discussions dwelled over the methodological problems. A somewhat different strategy emerged from the one outlined above. The team retained the idea that the ultimate aim of empirical research was that of formulating and testing hypotheses. However, we came to think differently about the forming of conceptual frameworks. Rather than deriving them from thought experiments and research, we decided to let the empirical material generated by the parallel case studies in England and The Netherlands speak for itself. Of course, this was only possible within limits. A minimum amount of conceptual order was imposed from the start, otherwise we might have got lost or, more likely, introduced assumptions without being fully aware of them (Thomas et al, 1983).

This is standard in exploratory research. But something else occurred also, stemming from our engagement with what we experienced. It resulted in questions raising themselves in our minds. Was it right that there was departure from statutory plans? Such departures occur on a massive scale in Dutch planning and raise serious issues about its efficacy. Planners react in a manner which varies from frustration to cynicism. Some of that feeling rubbed off on us.

We asked ourselves whether, by deviating from plans previously conceived, people had acted reasonably. Answering this question meant analysing their situations from their points of view. It involved reconstructing what decisionmakers and their professional advisers did and judging it in the light of some norm of reasonableness. The question is, what research strategy is involved? Obviously it is different from making recommendations based on empirical laws. The recommendation to be flexible when faced with uncertainty is clearly not based on such a law. To make it relevant, it is sufficient to demonstrate that *some* situations of uncertainty exist. This is an empirical fact, but not a law. As such it merely provides the occasion for recommending flexibility. The recommendation itself is a matter of *logical* analysis.

The process can be described as *methodological reflection*. "Methodological" because the problem was whether deviations from plans were done for correct reasons. "Reflection" because the thought process was different from empirical testing.

Methodological reflection seems an apt description of the research strategy of many planning authors. The classic study by Meyerson and Banfield (1955) demonstrates this. There, the experiences of Meyerson as adviser to the Chicago Housing Authority are interpreted by Banfield in the light of more general theories concerning planning, politics, and the public interest. The same applies to the work of the Institute for Operational Research (see chapter 2). Obviously, the cases are different, and the reconstruction takes place in the light of different theories. But the research strategy is still the same.

Case studies are common in the area of the methodology of science, where such studies likewise form the basis of methodological reflection. But in planning, there is also another typical form of research: *action research*. The reason for its prominence is twofold: first, it enables the planning methodologist to gain an excellent appreciation of practice. Much as methodologists of science, who keep in close touch with practicing scientists, so with planning methodologists—they benefit from intimate knowledge of practice. Second, action research is *the* way of working directly on the problems to which planning methodology addresses itself: improvements to the methods of planning. Such improvements depend on practitioners accepting recommendations made. Action research enables at least some of them to participate in methodological reflection themselves. Their example might induce others to adopt recommendations.

This is why methodological reflection is an appropriate method in planning research aimed at improving planning practice. Its contribution to this aim is more direct than that of the formation of an empirical planning theory. Hence the title of this paragraph: "empirical planning theory—a digression?" The answer is affirmative.

1.3 The core issue of *Planning Theory*, methodological and philosophical

The shift from planning theory to planning methodology stems from debates mentioned in the Acknowledgement. The one involving Reade will be described in chapter 9, in the review of my normative planning theory. The second debate centred on whether it was appropriate to stick to rationality in the light of the manifest failure of planning practice to approach this ideal, or whether rationality had thus been invalidated as a guide to planning. The critics in this case had, in common with Reade, their invocation of Popper—they claimed that rationality had been *falsified*.

The answer is that rationality is a methodological principle for decisionmaking on *a par* with falsification for empirical hypotheses and, as such, is *not* subject to falsification. This proposition will be developed—and modified—in chapter 6. In formulating it, I have been greatly encouraged by Popper's reply to Lakatos's question, "Under what conditions would you give up your demarcation criterion?"

"A question that I am almost regularly asked by intelligent students on their first acquaintance with my work is the following: 'But is your own theory of falsifiability (and of scientific method in general) falsifiable?' Now while this is a very natural question, it should not be asked by anybody familiar with my work. For the answer is that my theory is not empirical, but methodological or philosophical, and it need not therefore be falsifiable." (Popper, 1974b, page 1010)

Demanding, as these critics did, that rationality as the guiding principle underlying my *Planning Theory*, should be subject to empirical tests is equally incorrect. This applies also to Scott and Roweis's (1977) invoking Popper in their criticism of normative planning theory, as represented by myself, amongst others:

"... mainstream theory appears not so much to be incorrect as it is simply trivially true. For example, assertions that the planning process involves various forms of goal formulation, evaluation, implementation and control, learning, and all the rest, are no doubt true, but they are also plainly vacuous ... Quite simply, and to put the matter in Popperian terms, mainstream theory is structured for minimum rather than maximum refutability." (Scott and Roweis, 1977, page 1110)

As Los (1981, page 81) also points out, to demand that statements about how to proceed in planning should meet the test of falsifiability means applying the wrong criterion.

That Scott and Roweis do exactly this is underlined by their making the same point not once, but twice. Thus, elsewhere they attack conventional planning theory for "... positing formal and linguistic definitions of planning that have a purely *a priori* or nominalistic character". One of their objections is that "... it is difficult to think of any empirical test that in principle might refute any one of them" (Scott and Roweis, 1977, page 1098). Now, definitions are not usually subjected to falsification. Also, a mere look at the definitions which they criticise—planning as a goal-oriented process; planning as the application of rational decisionmaking procedures; planning as promoting human growth—shows that they express normative ideas. It is these which Scott and Reweis wish to subject to empirical tests, like hypotheses would be subjected to empirical tests. This is the same as Lakatos has demanded that Popper should do, evoking the reply quoted above.

Camhis's (1979, page 47) strictures against Popper not allowing his piecemeal social engineering to be tested (see chapter 3) are equally misconceived. Nevertheless, those who have raised the issue of the falsifiability of rationality deserve my thanks for having put me onto a useful track.

It has led me to identify my core concern as *methodological*. Next to planning methodology, it relates to *philosophical foundations of planning* concerning the nature of humans and society. I am finally also interested in *practice theory*: schemes, ideas, informed guesses relating to how the practice of planning might be brought more in line with methodological prescriptions and philosophical ideas. In outlining the first and the second of these, as I see them now, I gladly admit to having been influenced by Karl Popper. The third is represented by the work of the 'IOR-School', discussed in chapter 2.

If we were to make a fresh start in formulating the core of planning methodology in a Popperian vein, how would we proceed? We would seek to identify the *problem* which planning methodology should solve. Naturally, it would have to be a *methodological* problem. Concerning empirical research, Popper (1959) gives this account of the task of methodology, or what he calls the logic of scientific discovery:

"I suggest that it is the task of the logic of scientific discovery, or the logic of knowledge, to give a logical analysis of this procedure; that is, to analyse the method of the empirical sciences." (page 27)

He then goes on to ask: "What are these 'methods of the empirical sciences'? And what do we call 'empirical sciences'?" (ibid). Likewise, we should ask: "What are the 'methods of planning' and what do we call 'planning'?"

Now, the meaning of terms is ultimately a matter of agreement. I can only state what I mean by planning, hoping that those interested in similar problems might join me in my explorations. Thus, my view of planning (explained at more length in chapter 2) is that of an activity aiming at *correct decisionmaking concerning future courses of action.* It results in statements of intent, or *decisions.* Raising the issue of planning methodology means asking questions about the *rules to be applied to statements of intent, or decisions,* so that one can accept or reject proposals for good reasons. As in empirical research, these rules are *standards* concerning the *procedures by which proposals are to be judged.* This means we need planning methods for meeting these requirements. Indeed, many planning methods directly relate to rationality as here defined.

Now, if we were to attempt to solve this problem in the spirit of Popper, what would the answer be? As far as empirical research is concerned, Popper proposes a central rule: that only such statements should be admitted as scientific which can be falsified and which have, as yet, withstood stringent tests:

> "My criterion of demarcation will accordingly have to be regarded as a *proposal for an agreement or convention.* As to the suitability of any such convention opinions may differ; a reasonable discussion of these questions is only possible between parties having some purpose in common. The choice of the purpose must, of course, be ultimately a matter of decision, going beyond rational argument." (Popper, 1959, page 37; see also chapter 4)

What criterion can we offer as a proposal for an agreement concerning the central rule for planning methodology? Plainly, the problem is different from that of empirical research and, therefore, the convention will need to be different also. My proposal in chapter 6 will be that rationality is a rule for distinguishing correct decisions from ill-founded ones. To be more specific, decisions should be accepted only if they can been shown to be superior to their alternatives, judged against whatever goals are deemed to be relevant.

I am going to argue the case for accepting this proposal later on. There I shall also rectify my previous statement (Faludi, 1983; 1985) that rationality is the *exact* equivalent of the falsification criterion—this is not so. The purpose of outlining the case here is merely to identify previous arguments I now regard as methodological. There, I put these ideas in different terms, but there is no difference of substance. I say about the 'rational planning process':

> "... in presenting proposals ... , the proponents of substantive policies imply that they have gone through a rational thought process. The planning literature calls this the rational planning process of going through generation of alternatives, evaluation, and choice based on that evaluation.

Proponents of policies invoke this rational planning process because presenting an argument means to reconstruct and communicate a conclusion in such a way that somebody else is led to draw the same inference." (Faludi, 1984, page 30).

The methodological nature of my argument is evident, in particular where I quote Gould (1971) immediately after, that rationality is

"... a shorthand way of pointing out ... the ... standards which I and others appeal to when we try, individually or collectively, to give our 'reasons' in a clear and demonstrable form." (page 36)

As regards philosophical reasons for accepting rationality as a methodological rule for decisionmaking, again I take as my starting point Popper's argument concerning the reasons for accepting his demarcation criterion for scientific statements.

At first glance it is surprising to hear Popper describing the falsification criterion as a proposal for an agreement, and thus ultimately a question of "... value judgements and predilections ..." (Popper, 1959, page 38). The full reasoning behind this is to be found in *The Open Society and its Enemies* where he broadens this to saying that the rationalist attitude itself is a matter of making a moral choice:

"The rationalist attitude is characterized by the importance it attaches to argument and experience. But neither logical argument nor experience can establish the rationalist attitude; for only those who are ready to consider argument or experience, and who have therefore adopted this attitude already, will be impressed by them." (Popper, 1966, 1st edition 1945, page 230)

But Popper is still prepared to argue for rationalism:

"... arguments cannot determine such a fundamental moral decision. But this does not imply that our choice cannot be helped by any kind of argument whatever ... it is most helpful to analyse carefully the consequences which are likely to result from the alternatives between which we have to choose. For only if we can visualize these consequences in a concrete and practical way, do we really know what our decision is about; otherwise we decide blindly." (page 232)

In chapters 6 and 7, I shall return to this statement of Popper's. It will give us a clue to the Popperian demarcation criterion for justifiable decisions: consequentialism.

A few pages further down, Popper analyses the consequences of irrationalism therefore as follows:

"The irrationalist insists that emotions and passions ... are the mainsprings of human action. To the rationalist's reply that, though this may be so, we should do what we can to remedy it, ... the irrationalist would rejoin

... that this attitude is hopelessly unrealistic. For it does not consider the weakness of 'human nature' ....

"It is my firm conviction that this irrationalist emphasis upon emotion and passion leads ultimately ... to an appeal to violence and brute force as the ultimate arbiter in any dispute ... This tendency is very much strengthened by another ... which also is in my opinion inherent in irrationalism, namely, the stress on the inequality of men ...

"... This fact is connected with its emphasis upon emotions and passions; for we cannot feel the same emotions towards everybody ... The division between friend and foe is a most obvious emotional decision ...

"... Now, the adoption of an anti-equalitarian attitude in political life ... is just what I should call criminal." (pages 233–236)

Popper's disapproval of inequality is accompanied by an equally strong predilection for the equality of men as the basis of rationalism:

"This latter attitude with its emphasis upon argument and experience, with its device I may be wrong and you may be right, and by an effort we may get nearer to the truth, is ... closely akin to the scientific attitude. It is bound up with the idea that everybody is liable to make mistakes, which may be found out by himself or by others, or by himself with the assistance of the criticisms of others ... Thus a rationalist ... will reject all claims to authority ... we have not only to listen to arguments, but we have a duty to respond, to answer, where our actions affect others. Ultimately, in this way, rationalism is linked up with the recognition of the necessity of social institutions to protect freedom of criticism, freedom of thought, and thus the freedom of man." (pages 237–238)

These philosophical mainsprings of rationalism are the sources from which I also draw. This is particularly so where I describe the rationale of planning theory as promoting human growth (pages 39–52). This idea—which has been misunderstood more than once—simply means that planning increases the range and quality of our interventions, and that it involves learning, not only about our environment, but also about ourselves. Thus, human growth is a product and a process (pages 40–41). This concept of planning is similar to Popper's view of science leading to growth and progress:

"I assert that continued growth is essential to the rational and empirical character of scientific knowledge, that if science ceases to grow, it must lose that character." (Popper, 1963, page 215)

Even if rational planning does lead to human growth so defined, the question may still be legitimately asked as to *why* one should strive for it.

The reason lies in a Promethean view of man:

"Because growth ... also means self-guidance, this concept incorporates a view of man as gaining mastery over himself by power of his faculty of reason." (Faludi, 1984, page 45)

Similarly, Popper's *The Open Society and its Enemies* ends by saying:

"Instead of posing as prophets we must become the makers of our fate ... And ... when we have given up worrying whether or not history will justify us, then one day we may even justify history, in our turn. It badly needs justification." (Popper, 1966, page 280)

Above all, Popper has been quoted above as saying that the choice for or against what he calls rationalism is ultimately a moral choice. In the same manner, whether we wish to pursue human growth or not is ultimately a matter of choice also:

"In addition to having reasons what is needed is the optimism required to face up to the perpetual challenge which human growth poses: the challenge to pursue human growth relentlessly, and to fight obstacles of growth, wherever they may be; the challenge to abandon or check certain types of growth when they develop pathological aspects, however dear they may be to one's heart; the challenge of facing the anxieties involved in making decisions in the pursuit of growth; the challenge of sharing responsibility for mankind's future. It also requires faith in man's ability, and in particular in his faculty of reason." (Faludi, 1984, page 48)

In summary, then, my claim is that (1) the core argument of *Planning Theory* is methodological in nature, methodology being understood in a Popperian sense, and (2) its philosophical roots are the same as Popper's— a secular view of man as the maker of himself. But I quite admit that my concern at the time, also to point the way towards a positive theory of planning, has clouded the issue.

1.4 What to expect of planning methodology?
Popper's distinction between a "context of justification" and a "context of discovery" helps in clarifying expectations concerning planning methodology.

Methodology relates to how propositions (plans, scientific arguments) can be justified—and also criticised. How they come about, which psychological processes are involved—these are different issues. Or, as Popper states in the introductory chapter of *The Logic of Scientific Discovery*:

"... I must first make clear the distinction between the *psychology of knowledge* which deals with empirical facts, and the *logic of knowledge* which is concerned only with the logical relations." (Popper, 1959, page 30)

The difference is as follows: the logical analysis of scientific knowledge concerns only

"... questions of *justification or validity* ... Its questions are of the following kind. Can a statement be justified? And if so, how? Is it testable? Is it logically dependent on other statements? Or does it perhaps contradict them? In order that a statement may be logically examined in this way, it must already have been presented to us." (page 31)

I conclude that methodology cannot give guidance to what Popper terms "thought processes". His concern is with the logic of testing, that is, that statements purporting to be scientific, wherever they come from, should be submitted to stringent attempts to falsify them. Likewise, my concern is that decisions should be defensible in the light of some agreed standard. Although, when writing *Planning Theory* I had not fully assimilated this distinction, I nevertheless wrote:

"Planning may ... be defined as deciding on a course of action by satisfying oneself that it is possible to present one's choices in a form which could have resulted from a rational planning process, even if this has not actually been the case. Much as in science ... the effort of presenting a course of action in this way has the advantage of facilitating criticism and of establishing an unambiguous basis for agreement or conflict." (Faludi, 1984, page 38)

This view of what is commonly called (misleadingly) "the rational planning process" conforms to Popper's view of science:

"Insofar as the scientist critically judges, alters, or rejects his own inspirations we may, if we like, regard the methodological analysis undertaken here as a kind of 'rational reconstruction' of the corresponding thought processes. But this reconstruction would not describe these processes as they actually happen: it can only give the logical skeleton of the procedure of testing." (Popper, 1959, pages 31–32)

Quite often, rationality is misunderstood as a *behavioural* prescription. But rationality is a standard for critically assessing decisions once they have been made: a decision rule. How decisions are in fact made has no bearing on it. The way of criticising rules for decisionmaking is to show that they do *not* achieve what they are meant to achieve for reasons of *logic*. An even better criticism would be to show that there are *alternative* rules for identifying correct decisions. This is what many critics fail to do. In chapter 11, I shall outline such an alternative. It may represent a serious challenge to my approach to planning methodology which nobody has posed so far.

At this point I depart slightly from Popper though. In a collection of articles on *The Philosophy of Karl Popper* (Schilpp, 1974), Medawar (1974)

claims that it is the task of methodology to find out what scientists do, or
should do (page 287). Popper replies by drawing attention to the
distinction between the context of justification and of discovery as outlined
above, but he takes it further in saying when he would recant his view on
its usefulness:

> "I am inclined to say that we should attempt to find out what they
> [scientists—AF] ought to do. This 'ought' is not a matter of ethics, of
> course (though ethics comes in too) but rather the 'ought' of a
> hypothetical imperative. The question is: 'How should we proceed if
> we wish to contribute to the growth of scientific knowledge?' And the
> answer is: 'You cannot do better than proceed by the critical method
> of trial ... and ... error ...' I do not think that we should turn to the
> (sociological) question of what scientists actually do or say, except
> perhaps to refute certain competing answers ...
> I do not think that the theory of knowledge, or of scientific knowledge,
> is ... an empirical science, and testable or falsifiable in the sense in
> which, I hold, empirical theories are testable.
>   Yet I can conceive of empirical circumstances which would lead me
> to revise my theory of science. If, say, drinking coffee ... could be
> shown to stimulate the output ... of successful scientific theories ..., then
> this, I admit, would force me to give up my views ..." (Popper, 1974b,
> page 1036)

The example is extreme. Drinking coffee may not have such an effect.
But the context in which people work does have an influence on their
creativity. This is well known from organisation theory. From the
planning literature we know that the distribution of power, the structure of
organisations and political styles do influence the output of planning
agencies. The situation is even such that some Dutch authors—Van der
Cammen (1979), Kreukels (1980; 1982), and Bussink (1980)—plead for
integration between methodology and social science disciplines, offering
explanations of organisational and political behaviour. Now, it is not
obvious what integration could mean. But it is certainly possible to draw
on these disciplines.

For instance, from political science we learn that it is often useful *not*
to think of one unitary decisionmaker but to attend to conflicts. From
sociology we learn that our perspectives influence our thoughts. From
social psychology we hear about the importance of group size. So these
disciplines explain why problems are complex. Also, they assist in
formulating the conditions under which creative solutions to them are
more likely to be found.

In this way, it is useful to take cognizance of the various social sciences
concerned with the context of planning. However, their findings must be
translated into terms which are relevant to the level of argument in
methodology.

There is a further sense in which methodology does have a bearing on what happens in practice. Neither the falsification of hypotheses nor rational decisionmaking are straightforward. Considerable ingenuity is required. In the process, we use methods as routinised ways of solving recurring problems in the application of methodological rules. In planning, there are methods for the systematic generation and evaluation of alternatives. More recently, uncertainty management and monitoring methods have been added. Each one brings a facet of rationality into practice. In a manner of speaking, it helps to fill rationality in with the particulars at hand. In terms of the following chapter, we might say it helps to provide elements of the definition of the decision situation. In this way, planning methodology does inform what planners do. Indeed, this is its purpose: to inform planners of how to take correct decisions. The strategic choice approach (to be discussed briefly in chapter 2) is the result of attempts to develop a practicable way of conducting planning, taking account of the real situation in which it takes place. It is what I have termed a practice theory in the previous paragraph. As such, the 'IOR-School' and I go further than Popper would probably find interesting.

1.5 The plan for the book
The next chapter will give my current decision-centred view of planning, which is based on rationality as a methodological rule. Chapter 3 is devoted to works by planning writers referring to Popper. They present a picture which is far from coherent, as far as the implications of his thoughts are concerned.

Thus, it is necessary to go back to Popper's work and see what is relevant to planning methodology. This is what Part 2, chapters 4 and 5 are about. Chapter 6 forms the centrepiece of this book. It compares falsification with rationality. Chapter 7 culls building blocks from Popper's writing for a decision-centred planning methodology. Chapter 8 concentrates on Popper's notion of a "World 3" and gives a view of planning as the manipulation of symbols leading to the exercise of a form of "plastic control" on action. Chapter 9 shows my previous normative planning theory to be in accord with Popperian thinking.

Part 3, Conclusions, gives a summary in chapter 10. Chapter 11 indicates areas of possible criticism of Popperian planning methodology, the most challenging one being based on a theory of ethics opposed to Popper's and my consequentialism.

The decision-centred view of planning

This chapter introduces my *decision-centred view of planning*. I relate how I have come to formulate it, and locate it with respect to others.

First, the view of planning as revolving around decisions will be discussed. Thereupon, the evolution of this view will be traced, cumulating in a systematic presentation. Finally, the argument will be put into a wider context of ongoing discussions, not only in the field of planning theory but of operational research as well. This will all be brief because, one day, I hope to write another book on the decision-centred view of planning.

2.1 Decisions, decisions

Planning results in new *activities*, or in changes of ongoing ones. Its effect must be measured in terms of its influence on activities, therefore—there is no other way in which planning can have effect. (Of course, the effect of planning may also be learning. But that, too, derives its ultimate justification from its effect on activities.)

Planning concerns *future* activities and cumulates in *decisions*, which form the occasions when we declare our intentions. Now, private actors need not always account for their decisions; public authorities *must* do so. That government must be accountable is one of the most fundamental ideas of our times. But increasingly, private actors are also expected to account for their decisions.

The agendas of public meetings show a great variety of decisions. Many have a bearing on the environment: the voting of funds for the preparation of plans, the purchase of land, the execution of works, and the granting of compensation to those adversely affected. Likewise, powers of control prevent undesirable activities from occurring: cutting trees, erecting factories next to residential areas, destroying historic monuments, etc. Typically, each decision is laid down in a document stating the intent of the decisiontaker and providing a justification, however crude, in terms of purpose, powers, and resources. Its aim is to show that the proposal is for the correct decision to be taken. Environmental planning relates to a whole stream of such decisions concerning the development of the environment.

Of course, decision documents are no more than the tip of an iceberg. Proposals evoke debates. The opposition on the Council questions their wisdom, and the majority party defends them. Outside interests are aroused and try to influence decisions. Research is done, memos are written, negotiations occur, threats are exchanged, interest-groups withdraw their cooperation, funds and emotional energy are spent. All this is decisionmaking. On the face of it, none of this has much to do with the justification of decisions in a sense which would remind us of the justification of scientific propositions.

But, behind the facade of argument and conflict we discern a clear purpose. It is to search for an adequate wording of a proposal. As with science, decisionmaking is guided by rules. These make out what is, and what is not, acceptable.

Obviously, the rules must be so designed as to make decisionmaking into a useful exercise. Discussions *about* these rules take place on a higher plane than the discussions *within* these rules. In this book I talk about rules.

The reader will not be surprised to hear that rationality as presented in *Planning Theory* is the rule which I propose should be followed. This will concern us further in this chapter; in chapter 6, I shall argue that it is a Popperian rule.

2.2 The genesis of the decision-centred view of planning

Since publishing *Planning Theory* I have been profoundly influenced by the 'IOR-School'. Faludi and Mastop (1982) relate how this has come about, at the same time indicating why, contrary to impressions created by its work, this school adheres to rationality much as I do.

Shortly after the publication of *Planning Theory* I initiated the comparison of local planning and implementation in England and The Netherlands referred to previously. Initially I hoped the comparison might be directed to testing the hypotheses developed in *Planning Theory*. The expectations of the remainder of the research team were perhaps less specific, but we certainly hoped to move towards formulating an empirical theory of the procedural type. This has been described in chapter 1, together with how it departed from my original ideas. There, I also said that many of the questions raised I now regard as planning methodological.

For example, the fact that, in Leiden, statutory plans were honoured more in the breach than in the observance reminded me of Friend and Jessop's remark:

"... the significance of any planning activity—no matter how far into the future it may set out to look—will depend on the guidance that it can give in the selection of appropriate courses of action to deal with current circumstances." (1977, 1st edition 1969, pages 110–111)

This reflects the pragmatism expressed in the principle underlying British administration of 'deciding cases on their merits'. The underlying philosophy of Dutch planning is the opposite: plans should be adhered to, otherwise 'legal certainty' might suffer. Both approaches represent extremes of what might be called a protoplanning theory. Now, the Dutch protoplanning theory forms a puzzling contrast to the widespread practice of deviating from plans. We began to think that, really, there was nothing inherently wrong with this. Plans are prior investments so as to improve action. (Later I was to talk about operational decisions—see below.) If plans cannot be implemented, so much the worse for them. There is no

reason why reasonable actions should not be taken because a prior plan
forbids them, or why unreasonable actions should be taken because the
plan prescribes them so.   These thoughts led me to explore flexibility
in planning on the lines of the 'IOR-School' then engaged in structure
planning inquiries (see Sutton et al, 1977).   This is a methodological
problem.

Rationality was not directly at stake here.   The issue arose only when I
embarked on more research on IOR-lines, aimed at spreading the strategic
choice approach which I considered a good practice theory (see chapter 1).
The problem then was how my commitment to rationality in planning,
expressed in *Planning Theory*, could be squared with strategic choice.

One might be excused for thinking that the two have little in common.
Friend and Jessop barely touch on rationality.   Rather, they draw attention
to *uncertainty* militating against rational choice.   Worse still, in the follow-
up, Friend et al (1974) enthusiastically adopt Lindblom's idea of mutual
adjustment (Lindblom, 1965), again something which seems to contradict
rationality in planning.   Also, the main protagonist of strategic choice
since, Hickling (1974; 1975), never tires of saying that it is a way of
expanding our understanding, but nothing like a sure method of finding
any 'optimal' solution, whereas the search for such a solution is exactly
what rational planning is about.   So, rather than expounding rational
planning methodology, the 'IOR-School' is being seen as offering an
alternative to it (see also the "paradigmatic debate" below).

Grappling with this problem has led me to formulate my decision-
centred view of planning.   It complements the agency-centred view
advanced by Friend and Jessop.   Briefly, Friend and Jessop say that the
"governmental system" is composed of agencies, each of which with

"... terms of reference which define ... the classes of situations with
which it has authority to deal ..." (page 120).

Their book then exposes three forms of uncertainty which they found
agencies became aware of in selecting appropriate courses of action in
practice, and of the mechanisms for reducing uncertainty.   My view
focuses on the deliberations of agencies.

This focus leads one to ask when an agency might be satisfied that it
could bring its deliberations to an end, for the time being anyway.
The reader will no doubt identify this as the methodological core-question
discussed in the previous chapter.   My answer is that explorations may be
halted if and when the agency is satisfied that it has found the correct—
rational—decision.

My claim is that this rule underlies both the "operational problems"
which Friend and Jessop identify (finding solutions, expressing preferences,
exposing latent uncertainties, selecting exploratory actions and selecting
immediate commitment; see pages 115–119) and their "technology of
choice".   Thus, Analysis of Interconnected Decision Areas (AIDA) serves

the systematic exploration of what they describe as the "policy-space" (page 115; below I refer to this as the "decision-situation"), so as to be certain of finding the best course of action.

Admittedly, the 'IOR-School' are reluctant to talk in terms of 'correct', let alone 'best', solutions. Nevertheless, optimalisation is implied, particularly in AIDA. Decision areas are so defined as to form an exhaustive set. Strategies include all feasible combinations of decisions, one from each decision area. When all have been evaluated, the one scoring highest must, by virtue of this procedure, be regarded as the best strategy.

Protesting that we cannot be sure that the strategy thus identified is indeed the best is useless. The 'IOR-School' show how we can either reduce, or live with, uncertainties. As in statistical decision theory, we can—and must—define the optimum with a view to the uncertainties remaining. Also, we must accept that our views as to the optimum might change with new information becoming available and new attitudes being formed. Nor is it an argument that "one man's meat is the other man's poison", so that no general optimum can be said to exist. The agency-centred view is so defined that strategies are formulated from subjective points of view, and it is only from such a point of view that there can be talk about an optimum.

It will be evident what a great source of inspiration the 'IOR-School' has been to me. Towards the end of this book, in chapter 10, I shall argue that their stance can easily be described as critical rationalist. In any case, combining the orientation of the 'IOR-School' towards action here and now, which had been a source of inspiration in my comparative research, with this emphasis on rationality as a methodological principle, I came to formulate the decision-centred view of planning. The next section gives a more formal account.

2.3 The decision-centred view presented

Basic to this view are two pairs of concepts. The first is that of *operational decisionmaking* and *planmaking*. The second is that of *cognition* and *volition*. Cognition stands for the generation of alternatives and the analysis of their consequences and volition for actors committing themselves to specific lines of thought and action.

To underline the pragmatic orientation of the decision-centred view, I start with the more concrete level of operational decisionmaking. Day in, day out, public authorities take scores of decisions, issuing permits, entering into contractual obligations, putting public works out for tender, etc. I describe such decisions as operational.

An operational decision is a pronouncement committing a decisiontaker to perform a certain activity.

Development can be viewed as an on-going stream of decisions. Developers decide to acquire land. Its owners decide to put it onto the market.

Investors decide to provide capital. Architects decide on the shape of
buildings. The authorities decide to grant subsidies and to give planning
permissions. They, too, take investment decisions: sewage and road
works, schools and parks. Finally, people decide to take up residence in
new housing, vacating some other property, etc, etc.

Why this emphasis on operational decisions? The reason lies in what
Hickling has once described as the "Willy Sutton principle", named after a
New York bank robber. When caught, he was asked why he was robbing
banks and promptly replied: "Because that's where the money is!"
Operational decisions entail commitments and use resources and affect the
lives of people. Once taken, they foreclose other options. The danger is
that important decisions cannot be taken any more as and when required.
This is because resources are scarce, attention needs to be focused on one
issue at a time, and precedents need to be watched.

Operational decisions are acts of volition. Where public authorities are
involved, their proposals to enter into commitments must be supported by
argument. This does not mean to say that individuals do *not* act
responsibly. Individuals may equally be called upon to account for their
decisions. Sometimes, they even put their motives into writing so as to
keep a record for the future. For public authorities though, this is of
paramount importance.

For decisions to become a matter of public concern and criticism,
proposals must be publicly announced. In this way, *standards* can be
applied to them. Think about any ordinary decision requiring some
deliberation, for example whether to change jobs. In it, standards play
their part. This is even more true for discussions held in the public arena.

Considerations might concern the relations of the decisions in question
to other decisions, past, present, and future. Does the intended job square
with the decision taken previously to move house, and with that taken on
the doctor's advice to take things easier? Does the public authority's
decision to execute road works still allow it to fulfil its promise to build a
swimming pool? Clearly, some thinking is needed before such questions
can be answered—if, indeed, they *can* be answered. Many of them are
surrounded by considerable *uncertainty*.

Planning is simply the attempt to do this thinking systematically. As
regards husband and wife, a number of evening conversations on their
future, given the prospect of a new job, will usually suffice. But an
authority is under an obligation to demonstrate that it knows what it is
doing. It must make statements concerning the overall context within
which it takes its decisions. Public authorities therefore formulate and
adopt budgets, land-use plans, and other documents stating their policy.

The accountability of public authorities for their operational decisions is
the most fundamental norm from which the decision-centred view of
planning starts. How can one account for one's decisions? There must be

a general rule for answering this question, to which all those concerned can refer. Obviously, my proposal is to regard rationality as such a rule.

A decision is rational, if it results from an evaluation of all alternatives in the light of all their consequences.

It will be evident that this is a rule for *assessing* decisions once they have been formulated. Nothing is assumed about the process by which the decision has been formulated.

To be able to meet the requirements of rationality, one must *know* all feasible alternatives and their expected consequences. But in dynamic situations, the identification of consequences is difficult. Add to this that their evaluation implies attaching weights to them. Also, any evaluation bears the stamp of whoever has the ultimate say. In the case of public authorities, many questions arise about the manner in which various interests are reflected in the authority's decisions. Nevertheless, in principle, public authorities can be held accountable by various interests. Many evaluation methods attempt to deal with this problem. Their outcome is the object of political conflict. Since this is even more true for planmaking, I shall defer the discussion of this topic until later.

Difficulties notwithstanding, every effort must be made to identify alternatives and to evaluate their consequences. They add up to what I call the definition of the decision-situation:

A definition of the decision-situation is a description of the alternatives which a decisiontaker has with respect to a certain decision, together with their expected consequences weighed in the light of his/her values.

Seen in this way, the definition of the decision-situation embodies all that one must know before taking a decision. It forms the essential premise of any rational decision. In a manner of speaking, it represents a complete image of the world as seen by the decisiontaker at the moment of being confronted with it. The definition is subjective, as well as time-specific. Limitations on his/her freedom of choice are taken into account by including only those alternatives which he/she is both able and willing to consider. Here, the pragmatic orientation of the decision-centred view comes to the fore yet again. Limitations of knowledge may even lead to the rationality-rule itself being modified so as to minimise the risk of error. Many such variations have been proposed in statistical decisionmaking. They fall under the more general heading of uncertainty management, but need not concern us here.

Limitations arising from power constellations must also be taken into account. They prestructure definitions of decision-situations. Also, one takes account of only those consequences which one deems to be relevant. This is the only way in which we may conceive of *all* alternatives being evaluated in the light of *all* their consequences. Thus, defining decision-situations involves many decisions in its turn. Again, this will be discussed below in relation to planmaking.

Preparing every one of the operational decisions of public authorities in the way described above is impossible. Consequences of decisions are most diverse. They extend far beyond the area of competence of operational decisiontakers. As indicated, there is the danger that decisions will conflict with each other, and such consequences must also be figured out. This requires us to formulate *frameworks for operational decisions*. This is what a plan is, nothing more and nothing less.

In focusing on plans, the level of argument changes to sets of individual decisions viewed in combination. The adoption of a plan concerning such a set is a *planning decision*. It must be taken in the same manner as operational decisions.

In this, the reader will recognise Friend and Jessop's ideas. But I put more emphasis on frameworks as prior investments. In common with Friend and Jessop (1977, pages 110–112), I distinguish between two sorts of statements within plans: policy statements and programmes. This will figure in chapter 5, where Popper's theory of intervention is discussed in terms of this distinction.

The need to account for planning decisions means that in planmaking, too, the advantages and disadvantages of all alternative proposals need to be considered before opting for one. Rationality again applies as a norm. A definition of the decision-situation is an equally necessary premise. But it is a more complex affair, because planning decisions relate to sets of operational decisions. In other words, the volitional act, which the adoption of a plan also represents, presupposes much intricate cognitive work.

This gives rise to even more problems than is the case when defining operational decision-situations. The consequences of a plan must be calculated via the effects of the plan on operational decisionmaking and action. So, cause-and-effect-chains become longer, and uncertainty increases: there is uncertainty as to whether operational decisiontakers will implement a plan as they should. This quite apart from the inherent uncertainty attached to any prediction of consequences for the environment and people's lives.

For instance, the adoption of a green belt policy in order to prevent individual settlements from merging and so losing their identity is based on the following: (a) such a policy prevents development in designated areas, (b) preventing settlements merging with one another indeed preserves their identity. Green belts are under constant pressure, however, simply because they are adjacent to urban areas, and whether something as elusive as the identity of settlements depends on their physical separation remains open to doubt. In this way, the evaluation of a green belt policy involves a chain of, more or less uncertain, expectations concerning its consequences.

Add to these uncertainties the large number of alternatives and consequences, and the need to attach weights to them, and the desire comes naturally for great selectivity in planmaking. Therefore, one must be grateful for any political signals, for any statement of a philosophy from which to define the decision-situation in planning. Otherwise, planmaking becomes a hopeless affair dealing with a hotchpotch of information which no conceivable planning agency has the capacity to assimilate.

Operational decisions and plans are similar. As we have seen, both are acts of volition. To take them in deliberate fashion means that one must take cognizance of the situation at hand. The distinction between volition and cognition is purely conceptual, of course. In reality, volition does not occur separately and after cognition, but occurs throughout decision-making or planmaking. Thus, the definition of the decision-situation is itself the result of choices concerning the range of alternatives and of consequences considered, including how they pertain to various interests. Simple distinctions, such as that between the preparation of plans by experts and their adoption by politicians, are insufficient, but this is where I let this matter rest for the time being. (But see chapters 5 and 9.)

Ultimately, problems in defining decision-situations stem from the nature of human knowledge. We are unable to grasp reality completely, let alone decision-situations involving considerations of an uncertain future. One reason is physiological. Information needed for action is stored in the so-called short-term memory. This is extremely limited in capacity. Potentially relevant information at our disposal needs to be reduced before it can be brought to bear.

Now, the principles involved in such a reduction can themselves *not* be derived from observations of reality. There is more than one way of perceiving reality. This is why definitions of decision-situations are subjective. They are themselves the results of a number of decisions. The subjective nature of definitions of decision-situations becomes evident when there is more than one actor involved, as is invariably the case in planning. Thus, an authority might think in terms of improving traffic flow in an inner-city area, whilst its inhabitants consider traffic as a hazard; the authorities might consider a slum as a potential area for expanding a shopping area, whilst the inhabitants see the housing as in need of rehabilitation, etc. Mutual adjustment of these views requires *negotiations.*

In negotiations, the partners can threaten each other by calling into question their respective definitions of the decision-situation. This is the painful experience of planners whose legitimacy in dealing with issues from an overall point of view (just think of comprehensive road proposals!) has been challenged. (A powerful actor may therefore conclude that negotiations are not worth his while. He will impose *his* definitions of decision-situations on others.)

How can we live up to the demands imposed by rationality? This rule does not seem to allow for any compromise. The answer is that we *take account* of existing limitations. They form, so to say, *part of* the definition of the decision-situation. In this respect, practice is often more advanced than theory. As the research on Dutch planning referred to above shows, exaggerated demands are simply ignored: in theory, all building permits should be issued in accordance with plans previously adopted, but in practice this requirement is flouted. In theory, statutory plans should be reviewed every ten years, but no such review is attempted unless there is an independent reason for doing so; etc, etc.

An important result of my decision-centred view has been the development of a cogent approach to flexibility (see Thomas et al, 1983). Briefly, flexibility may be seen as a response to the problem of bridging the gap, in terms both of organisational and temporal distance, between operational decisionmaking and planmaking. Time heals many wounds, it is said. It certainly removes some uncertainties. Also, the further down we go in organisational hierarchies, the more detailed the knowledge concerning operational decisionmaking. A recurrent answer to uncertainty is to delay and/or delegate decisions. This increases flexibility. But there are limits to the extent to which this can be done, beyond which the advantage of planning is lost. Since Popper's "World 3" concept has a bearing on this, the issue of flexibility will be developed in chapter 8.

This presentation of the decision-centred view of planning should allay any fear concerning the 'technocratic', or 'positivistic' connotations of rationality. The idea that it has anything to do with misconceived views of objectivity, or the common interest, and the like, should disappear. It takes account of the subjective nature of decisions and of the elusive one of any search for a common denominator of various interests. However, these difficulties relate to defining the situation to which the rationality rule applies. They do not suggest that this rule itself, straightforward as it is, needs to be modified. Therefore, I cannot help feeling that critics of rationality in planning might usefully redirect their attention to how decision-situations are defined, rather than to dwell over rationality. Rationality underlies their concern for broadening considerations in planning to include more, and more fundamental, issues.

2.4 Paradigmatic debates in planning methodology

Rules as to what planning is cannot be issued. Ultimately, as said before, the meaning of terms is a matter of agreement. Paradigmatic discussions are characterised by lack of agreement, therefore. This does not make them less interesting, but it is in the nature of paradigms that they throw up boundaries around areas of concern and separate believers from nonbelievers so that the struggle between them, far from being a mere scientific discussion, takes on some of the qualities of an interfaith conflict.

Planning theory is not alone in being faced with conflicts of this kind. There is a paradigmatic debate concerning approaches to decisionmaking, problemsolving, planning and design outside the field of environmental planning as well.

Thus, Dando and Bennett (1981) argue, following the views of Fay (1975; see also chapter 11) that operational research possesses three paradigms: official, reformist, and revolutionary. The official paradigm aims for certainty in decisionmaking based on substantial efforts in building models, calculating effects, etc. Ackoff's plea for moving away from this, what he calls the "predict-and-prepare" paradigm, towards one taking cognizance of uncertainty (see Ackoff, 1979a; 1979b) they describe as reformist. They foresee—not without regret—that it will carry the day, but their preference is for the revolutionary paradigm raising the issue of who is in control.

Readers more familiar with the literature of environmental planning than of operational research will be reminded of Harvey's distinction between revolutionary and counterrevolutionary science (see Harvey, 1973). Needless to say that, in these terms, both the official as well as the reformist view are counterrevolutionary. This suggests that there are two issues involved in Dando and Bennett's threefold distinction. There is the issue between the official and reformist paradigm concerning ways of going about finding solutions to problems. There is the second issue of who calls the tune.

Concerning the first issue, the paradigmatic change advocated by the reformist view really revolves not around optimality (rationality in terms of this book), as Ackoff, and Dando and Bennett in his wake, suggest, but around assumptions of the 'official' view of operational research (and of planning for that matter) concerning the nature of knowledge. According to Ackoff's "predict-and-prepare" paradigm, the assumption is clearly that, with the necessary effort, sound knowledge is to be had, and that action should be based on such knowledge. The step from knowledge to action is considered unproblematic. The optimal course of action flows from what one knows with certainty.

But the uncertainty of knowledge and the fact that there are choices involved in its generation and application rather suggest that the 'official' paradigm is not a serious proposition any more. At least it is not one that can be defended on methodological grounds. Also, the step from knowledge to action is considered unproblematic. I call this the *object-centred view of planning*. As in operational research, planning may equally well be approached from the angle of who is in control: the *control-centred view* (see also Faludi, 1982).

In this book, planning is rather seen as decisionmaking concerning future action: the *decision-centred view* presented earlier in this chapter. Knowledge concerning substantive issues and instruments of control is assumed to be available so that some decisions with a real impact on

important issues can be contemplated. The central question is how.
The advantage of this view lies in the affinity with the situation of
practising planners in the business of preparing decisions. It is towards its
methodological aspects that I direct my attention.

Radical theorists referred to in my Introduction argue that the control-
centred view of planning is of more relevance because it deals with the
function of planning in late capitalist society, and more in particular with
its limitations. To them, planning is the object of substantive social
science research aiming to understand it as embedded within urbanisation
and as reflecting the contradictions inherent in capitalism. From this point
of view, Scott and Roweis (1977) condemn other types of planning theory:

"... mainstream planning theory, as a set of analytical propositions about
the domain of planning, seems to be remarkably uninteresting from a
scientific point of view." (page 1114)

But Harris (1978) retorts that their theory

"... provides an easy way out of the difficulties of learning, practicing
and accommodating to planning. The tasks, the difficulties and the
processes of planning are imputed to the development tendencies of
society as a whole, and these tendencies are in turn explained by
standard Marxist concepts ..." (page 222).

One thing is certain: the control-centred view of planning does not
address itself to planning methodology. The choice between this perspective,
and one which does address issues of methodology, cannot be decided on
methodological grounds alone.

But the choice between an object-centred and a decision-centred paradigm
can be decided in such a manner. We may conclude unambiguously that
the first—identical with Ackoff's "predict-and-prepare" paradigm and
Dando and Bennett's official one—is not compatible with our understanding
of the nature of human knowledge. But in my view this does *not* affect
rationality as a rule, as Ackoff seems to suggest. It merely destroys the
assumptions that (a) we can achieve a form of understanding of the objects
of planning which is complete, certain, and objective in the sense of being
devoid of value-assumptions, (b) such understanding is a necessary and
sufficient condition of rationality in decisionmaking and planning. Since
none of these assumptions is involved in my advocating rationality as a
methodological rule—the definition of decision-situations has been
described as uncertain and bound by the perspectives of the actors
concerned—we must not shed the rationality-baby with the bathwater of
certainty in moving from one paradigm to the other.

Indeed, I question whether Ackoff, Friend and Jessop, and their
cotheorists are involved in a paradigm change at all. Rather, in developing
scientific approaches to problemsolving, decisionmaking, and planning,
they merely show us the way towards a more adequate understanding of

the methodology of science. Or is this what Dando and Bennett mean
when they describe a view like Ackoff's as 'reformist'?

2.5 Conclusions

In chapter 1, the problem of planning methodology has been identified as
finding rules for decisionmaking. This chapter has given the reasons for
focusing on *decisions*. They are the crucial elements in planning, including
what is commonly called implementation. But he who is not interested in
decisionmaking will find this view less appealing.

Before exploring the implications of Popperian methodology of science
for planning seen as evolving around decisionmaking, it is necessary to
review the works of other planning writers drawing on Popper. Mostly,
their understanding of Popper is quite satisfactory. What one must take
issue with is their notion, albeit implicit, of what planning methodology is
about. This may sound odd. After all, these are leading authors.
Alas, such is the state of planning methodological argument that there is
uncertainty, even about the issues to which it adresses itself!

Popper in the planning literature

In the Preface, I pointed out the attention paid to Popper in the literature on environmental planning. The aim of this chapter is to review this attention.

Two viewpoints exist. Some works refer primarily to Popper's *social philosophy*. A more substantial range of books and articles seeks to establish the relevance to planning of his *methodology of science*.

First, the references to social philosophy will be discussed. Mainly, this concerns Braybrooke and Lindblom's (1963) invocation of "piecemeal engineering" as a forerunner to their "disjointed incrementalism". Then, the works of Chadwick (1978), Dunn (1971), Gillingwater (1975) and Hart (1973; 1976), Camhis (1979), Taylor (1980), McConnell (1981), Heywood (1982) and Reade (1983) will be analysed. All of them refer mainly to Popper's methodology of science. Friedmann's (1977) critique of Popper's "World 3" concept stands apart in singling out an aspect of his late philosophy.

These works pay insufficient attention to the distinction between methodology of science on the one hand and of planning on the other (see chapters 1 and 2). This will greatly concern me in chapter 6, where I shall draw consequences of this distinction for my approach to planning methodology. From this my critique of the reception of Popper I shall conclude that (a) an overview is needed of Popperian philosophy and (b) its relevance to planning methodology must be reconsidered.

Unease about the reception which Popper gets in the planning literature arises out of my understanding of his work in conjunction with my view of planning methodology discussed above. As regards my understanding of Popper, this will have to wait. I take the reader through the literature first. My strategy is to make him/her wonder as to what Popperian philosophy really involves. In this way, I hope to prepare the ground for Part 2.

3.1 The reception of Popper's social philosophy

Popper's social philosophy as laid down in *The Poverty of Historicism* (1961, first published as two separate papers in 1944-1945) and *The Open Society and its Enemies* (1966, 1st edition 1945) formed part of what I like to term the *classic planning debate* (see Faludi, 1982). Other contributors were Lippmann (1937), Hayek (1962, 1st edition 1944), and Mannheim (1940), to name but a few. The debate had been sparked off by the example of Soviet and Fascist planning and concerned the merits of liberal democracy as against central planning. It mostly involved refugees from Nazi Germany. They had little difficulty in persuading people to reject Nazism. But the Soviets were allies. So, the fear was that the wave of sympathy for the heroic struggle of the Russian people might lull the West into believing that there was no fundamental difference as regards societal guidance in East and West. The extent of war-time planning in the West had blurred the distinction anyhow.

Even before World War II, Marxism evoked lively debates, not the least about its planning implications. Naturally, these concerned economic rather than environmental planning. Already during the economic crisis of the thirties, its liberal opponents warned against intellectual fascination with the idea of central planning. Their message continued to be that central planning would produce worse effects than the market, and that the dangerous road towards such a form of societal control should not be followed. *The Poverty of Historicism* argued so against Mannheim's famous work *Man and Society in an Age of Reconstruction* (1940). Hayek, in the *The Road to Serfdom* (1962), provided a searching critique of those who wanted to continue with a planned economy. Both writers objected to the manner in which decisionmaking was organised under regimes vesting supreme power in the state. This rigidly centralised form of planning they identified with planning as such, and thus a great opportunity for a debate on the manner of planning in a democratic society was lost. In a less heated atmosphere, perhaps a common ground might have emerged between Mannheim, Popper, Hayek, Lippmann, and others around a loose form of framework planning, or process planning, for none of the critics rejected the idea of planning as such, only that society should be managed according to a central blueprint.

Popper has never developed his views on planning beyond those expressed in the forties. He considers methodology of science to be his main field of interest (see his "Autobiography", 1974a; see also chapter 4). When asked to comment on planning, he tends to reiterate the same views. Thus, in the Foreword to a recent German textbook on environmental planning (Moewes, 1980), he points out that plans are rarely implemented and that most of them go wrong anyway, pleading for what the current literature describes as process planning. As in *The Poverty of Historicism* (1961), he upholds the approach of the engineer as an example of searching for, and learning from, mistakes. Yet he recognises the difficulties faced by planners who cannot experiment, and whose mistakes will emerge only in the future. Also, planners must try and anticipate the future, but their expectations can never be scientifically based (this being another idea drawn from his social philosophy). He ends by reflecting on the tradition of criticism in the arts and sciences, and on the theme of learning from mistakes. It is clear that he regards his social philosophy as most relevant for planning.

As indicated, this is echoed by the earlier references to his work in the current planning literature. Probably Braybrooke and Lindblom (1963, page 46) are the first to refer to Popper. Their work does not concern environmental planning, but is so widely referred to in this field that one cannot ignore it. They quote Popper's emphasis on the limitations of knowledge, and his argument that it precludes comprehensiveness in analysis.

They conclude that decisionmaking must take account of the experimental nature of policymaking, in which ends are as much adjusted to means as means to ends. Also, they follow his argument that one should concentrate on eliminating evil instead of pursuing goals (page 82).

This 'negative utilitarianism' has drawn the attention of planning writers, for instance Etzioni (1968, page 268), to whom we are indebted for having formulated the 'mixed scanning' strategy. Since it purports to surpass Braybrooke and Lindblom, it might have been interesting for him to reflect on whether it would get Popper's approval. As it stands, Etzioni's reference to Popper is of no further consequence for his work.

Needham (1971, page 318) picks up the same theme, arguing that "... planning should generally try to solve problems rather than achieve goals." But goals and problems stand in a symmetrical relationship to one another. In a joint paper (Needham and Faludi, 1973), we see the central issue, therefore, as not between goals and problems as the starting point but between collectivism and individualism (about which more shortly). So, I maintain that the shift which is said to have taken place in the seventies, from a goal-orientated to a problem-orientated approach to planning (see for example Drake et al, 1975) does not represent a departure from the previous manner of planning. An analysis of problems, if divorced from the societal decisionmaking process which alone explains how problems become *recognised* as issues, can be as abstract as goalsetting.

In a recent book, Needham (1982, page 8) clearly recognises that problem definition *is* a societal decisionmaking process. I no longer take issue with his starting from problems, therefore. My preference, as emphasised in chapter 2, remains for starting with an analysis of those *decisions* which one is, or might be, willing to contemplate in planning, recognising that each decision implies a definition of a problem. It is because of the fact that problems are socially defined that I have doubts about Needham's and Popper's methodological individualism.

More light is shed on this in Needham (1977). There, he bases his preference for methodological individualism on *The Open Society and its Enemies* (Popper, 1966). Individualists analyse social relations in terms of the interactions between individuals, collectivists do so in terms of social classes or organisations or societies. Now, Needham disclaims that—as is often argued—individualism implies that sociology can be reduced to psychology. Also, "... the individualist approach does not rule out talking about collectivities ..." (page 4). Much as Popper (see 1966, volume 2, page 97), he accepts that analyses use a mixture of individualistic and collectivistic concepts. Therefore, his—and Popper's—individualism does not seem methodological but ethical. This comes across where Needham says:

"... in my opinion, people are more important than groups, and ... to analyse at a level of groups is to court the danger of forgetting about, or being insensitive to, individuals." (1977, page 4)

I recognise this, but at root this is not an issue of methodology (see also chapter 9). Rather it concerns how decision-situations must be defined and in particular whether the definition of decision-situations must always in the end refer to the effects of decisions on individuals.

In the same work, Needham (1977) makes another attractive suggestion. It concerns the use of what Popper has termed the "zero method" in *The Poverty of Historicism*. Needham presents this as a general method for investigating urban policymaking. Unfortunately, he is not very precise in describing the application of this method. He begins by saying that it is a method "... which assumes that politicians and public officials are rational" (page 160), only to say a few lines further down that we "... do not need to assume that they act thus self-consciously or even successfully—only that we can use a model of rationality for understanding and explaining the actions of people in public positions. The alternative assumption is that such people act willfully, or whimsically, ..." (1977, page 160).

What Needham should rather have said is that the zero method is one which enables us to appreciate how an actor should decide in accordance with his or her own best interests, irrespective of how he/she does decide in actual fact. The method provides a critical yardstick for the evaluation of actual behaviour. Such is the way in which Popper envisages it being used. He even proposes that it is *the* method of the social sciences concerned with understanding human behaviour in specific situations. In chapter 7, we shall see that this involves applying rationality.

3.2 The reception of Popper's philosophy of science

Braybrooke and Lindblom, and Needham (and my reply to him) still relate in the main to the theme of the classic planning debate: the extent to which planning, in the sense of societal control over individual actions, can be justified.

The modern planning debate originated in the United States. There, societal planning had become anathema after World War II, and planners who, during the New Deal, had been involved in the setting up of the National Resources Planning Board and similar institutions turned to less controversial fields like environmental planning. In this field a fruitful research tradition on planning theory emerged. Many links were forged with another activity above suspicion, business planning. The influence should be noted of the work of Barnard (1938) and Simon (1976, 1st edition 1945) on the famous Chicago planning programme from which so many ideas have emanated (see Perloff and Friedmann, 1957). Similarly, operational research, systems analysis, and cybernetics have left their marks. Since all these are deeply concerned with the application of scientific method to problemsolving, decisionmaking, and even politics, it is not surprising to find that, where references are made to Popper, more and more attention is paid to his methodology of science.

Chapter 3

3.2.1 G A Chadwick, *A Systems View of Planning*

Chadwick (1978, 1st edition 1970, page 66) in his now classic work gives an account of Popper's theory of objective knowledge as proceeding from problems *via* tentative solutions to error elimination and to the revision of the original solution. He argues that in applied research this process becomes modified by the introduction of modelling and systems concepts. The discussion cumulates in a "... rational model of systemic planning, derived from scientific method" (figure 4.3, page 68; for a whole range of criticisms—not all of them justified—see Camhis, 1979, pages 51-52).

Later, Chadwick introduces Popper's distinction between logical probability and verisimilitude:

"If we are to postulate future actions, clearly we must be able to form some image of what the future is going to be like. Now, of course, the future, in fact, cannot be predicted: we cannot know 'the truth' about the future until it has occurred, but we act as if we can foretell the future to some extent. This is because we tend to substitute for the idea of verisimilitude, of approximation towards the truth of a situation, the idea of probability of occurrence of certain events ... Karl Popper (1965) makes the distinction clearly: 'logical probability represents the idea of approaching logical certainty, or tautological truth, through a gradual diminution of informative content. Verisimilitude, on the other hand, represents the idea of approaching comprehensive truth. It thus combines truth and content while probability combines truth and lack of content.'" (Chadwick, 1978, page 155)

There follows a discussion of prediction in planning with no apparent relation to Popper's views. Surprisingly Chadwick retains probability, seemingly forgetting Popper's strictures against it.

In his chapter on "Satisfaction or optimisation?" Chadwick—drawing on *The Poverty of Historicism*—then puts forward a "rational incrementalism". He repeats Popper's criticism of blueprint planning and his account of engineering design, claiming that:

"... what appears to be holistic planning is in fact the summation of many incremental tests and operations. Popper is right, of course ... but his analogy is rather inappropriate: 'blueprint' engineering design is a much more bounded operation than 'social engineering' ... Thus, Popper's piecemeal social engineering is rather akin to disjointed incrementalism in both its strategy and its intention to base action on the consideration of the present (defective) situation rather than upon more distant goals; the latter aspect is an implicit recognition, of course, of the need for a lower-variety strategy, rather than one of too high a variety." (page 319)

Now, that engineering design is a more bounded operation than social engineering will hardly surprise Popper. As we shall see in chapter 5, his point is just that engineers use a piecemeal, experimental approach, and not an holistic one, the appearance of holism in engineering design notwithstanding. Also, the comparison between piecemeal engineering and disjointed incrementalism, plausible though it may seem, does not follow from the previous argument. Chadwick's final comment about low-variety and high-variety strategies requires elaboration. Instead, he launches into another discussion of piecemeal engineering. Apparently it leaves him uneasy:

"There may be situations in which the existing state of affairs is very undesirable, small changes will not achieve desired goals, and scientific methods have not confirmed the probable consequences of large incremental changes; here any change, even the continuation of existing policies, is a risk, and calculated risk becomes the most rational action." (page 319-320)

This implies criticism of Popper similar to that sometimes made against disjointed incrementalism as being conservative (see amongst others Etzioni, 1968, page 220). But Chadwick continues by criticising its opposite, Utopianism, in turn. It has "... a place in the setting of goals for society ...", but Utopias "... are not a substitute for rational methods ..." (page 320). Elsewhere, he is even more cautious as regards the Utopian tradition in planning, equating it with civic design and relegating it to "... the realm of aesthetics and art-criticism and appreciation only, not as an *essential* part of town planning as a social decision process" (page 353), thereby referring to Popper's attack on the "Platonic politician" who composes cities for their aesthetic satisfaction (see also chapter 4 below). But instead of any firm conclusion, he merely adds: "The point, at least, is worth debating."

Chadwick is intrigued by Popper. But too many questions remain unresolved. What is the exact nature of the analogy between Popper's theory of objective knowledge on the one hand and Chadwick's model of rational planning on the other? What about Chadwick's use of the concept of probability where Popper argues for verisimilitude? What, in the light of the above, is Chadwick's attitude towards Utopian and piecemeal engineering? But it is certain that Camhis's (1979, page 51) labelling of Chadwick as a Utopian is misleading. Chadwick expresses enough doubt about Utopianism to escape that verdict!

3.2.2 E S Dunn *Economic and Social Development*
By way of Friedmann's work (Friedmann, 1973), Dunn (1971) has been influential in developing our ideas about planning as learning by experiment. At the same time, he is the first of a number of authors who wrongly identify plans with hypotheses and/or implementation with testing them.

Dunn frequently invokes Popper, in particular his evolutionary view of knowledge (page 84). He relates the well-known quotation on letting hypotheses die instead of living beings, as is the case in biological evolution (see chapter 6). Also, he bases his "forms of adaptation" on the Popperian distinction between prophecy and prediction (page 115; see also pages 152 – 153). Furthermore, he quotes Popper on the impossibility of "laws of evolution" (page 126). Finally he develops the notion of an "evolutionary experiment" on the lines of piecemeal engineering (page 133; footnote page 136; see also page 269). It is his most important concept, as far as this study is concerned:

"Social learning involves more than the engineering of prophecy or the playing out of an optimum strategy in a stochastic game with fixed rules and objectives. Social learning is much involved with changing the 'name of the game'. At root, the learning process is manifest as an iterative exploratory series of experiments in social action. Although uncertainty ... remains an important element in the process, the conditional probabilities ... are made an object of deliberate, purposive modification. There is a direct normative component to this process that is supplied by human goals.

"We characterise this social learning process as evolutionary experimentation ... The concept is similar to one which Popper ... calls 'piecemeal problem solving', although Popper does not fully articulate the nature of the concept in its social context and, as will be apparent, does not treat the full scope of the process." (page 133)

Nowhere does Dunn spell out why he thinks that Popper does not treat the full scope of the process. Rather, he goes on to emphasise the nature of predictions as being "developmental hypotheses", which is uncontroversial as far as it goes. He declares that whether the performance of the social system will be modified so as to improve its efficiency,

"... is not known to be true on the basis of established deterministic laws. It is not an exercise in simple engineering design. Planning takes the form of conducting an experiment by embodying the new modes of behavior in the performance of the system. It can be viewed as testing the developmental hypothesis in action. If the developmental hypothesis is not falsified ... the novel mode of behavior will be reinforced and persist. If the results call the hypothesis in question, a new ... one will take its place ..." (pages 133 – 134).

One is left to wonder whether Dunn has fully assimilated Popper's views on experiments. The analogy with scientific experiments breaks down, simply because Dunn does not intend that social experimentation should proceed on the basis of established laws. Thus, when results contradict expectations, all manner of conclusions can be drawn. It need *not* mean that the underlying hypotheses are wrong.

Dunn recognises this when talking about classical and evolutionary experiments respectively:

"In physical systems classical science is concerned with the consistency and universality of relationships ...

"The social experiment that takes the form of the implemented plan is not subject to this kind of testing and does not seek to establish universal principles. It cannot because it is phenomenologically unique. At any time any functional social system displays a unique behavioral state ... The same planning experiment cannot be performed upon two identical systems. Furthermore, the object of the planning experiment is to change the performance of the system. One cannot return the system to its preexperimental state and retest the same experiment ... To achieve this, social problem solving engages in experimental tinkering with the system by subjecting it to a series of behavioral changes each of which is evaluated in terms of whether or not it improves the system's overall performance with respect to some desired goal or criterion of behavior. The fact that this mode of experimentation does not yield universal laws makes it no less scientific if it is consciously and objectively carried out and subjected to the test of performance." (pages 135 – 136)

Dunn develops his argument further by referring to Kuhn and Schon. This is not relevant to the treatment of critical rationalism in the planning literature.

The analogy between 'social experimentation' and 'piecemeal engineering' is uncontroversial, as far as it goes. That between science and planning is at best loose. Dunn compares the crucial experiment with the implementation of a plan—this is not correct. A plan can never be implemented twice; it is unique. This whereas repeatability is the whole point of experiments. Also, because of their uniqueness, attention should focus on the point in time when plans are adopted, and not when they are implemented. Lastly, it is correct to say that social experimentation can be as rigorous as scientific experimentation, but what exactly does this mean in Popperian terms? As we shall see below, and again in chapter 6, lack of attention to this issue is the crux with so many authors following Popper.

3.2.3 D Gillingwater and D A Hart, The 'Triple Helix'
Hart (1973; 1976) and Gillingwater (1975) develop a view of the planning process based on Popper's notion of the way in which organisms solve problems (see: "Of clouds and clocks", in Popper, 1973, 1st edition 1972) centering on the elimination of error. Also, like Chadwick, although

following Popper, they do not wholly adopt disjointed incrementalism:

> "... it is possible to reject both the fluid approach implicit in disjointed
> incrementalism and the cast-iron approach symbolized by the unitary
> Master Plan, and assert that there is at least one other way ... The
> third logically possible mode of planning ... views iterative planning as a
> spiral which seeks to serially and reciprocally relate image to reality
> within the context of induced, anticipated and unexpected change.
> Plans are necessarily probabilistic from this viewpoint because they
> have limited actual control over their environment and also because
> they are chronically short of reliable information ..." (Hart, 1976, page 23).

With Hart, Gillingwater (1975, pages 43–48) represents the planning
process as a triple helix "... mapping out the continuous interactions and
iterations between, respectively, policy problems, policy intent and policy
impact through time" (page 44). He then replaces the notion of a problem
by that of a problem area, signifying awareness that the very formulation
of a problem is a matter of choosing between an infinite number of
possibilities (see the previous discussion of Needham, 1982). He rightly
relates this to Popper's view of facts—and descriptions of problems—as
being theory-laden.

Also, both Hart and Gillingwater develop the theme of *plastic control* in
organisms. Gillingwater adds to these ideas by identifying what he terms
"the ideology of rational planning", not with Popper's stance (which he
describes as deductive-indeterminism), but with inductive-determinism, and
thus positivism.

The 'triple helix' view is a worthwhile attempt to come to terms with the
dynamic nature of planning, rich in suggestions, especially as regards the
implications of Popper's theory of problemsolving and his ideas of plastic
control in organisms. But what about Gillingwater's claim that rational
planning should be rejected as being positivist? This rests on the
arguments that the 'rational model'

> "... ties in quite neatly with the inductive approach to the philosophy of
> scientific method ... the stress on observations, facts and evidence are
> some of its critical, indeed distinguishing features. It therefore has
> significant and distinctive positivistic leanings ..." (Gillingwater, 1975,
> page 40).

But nothing in the 'rational model' which I propose suggests that one
should proceed inductively from facts to generalisations. Gillingwater's
charge of "positivism" simply does not hold.

3.2.4 M Camhis *Philosophy and Town Planning*
With Gillingwater, Camhis (1979) claims that rational-comprehensive
planning is equivalent to verificationism and logical positivism in the realm
of the methodology of science. At the same time he likens disjointed

incrementalism with falsificationism. This begins when Camhis describes
Popper's rejection of verificationism. He compares this with Simon
introducing the concept of satisficing—a "... major overall retreat ... in the
'rational' approach in planning" (page 32).

But Camhis does not succeed in demonstrating the link between
falsificationism and disjointed incrementalism. He starts by saying that the
relation between the two concepts is "... at once simple and complicated"
(page 37). Simple because of Braybrooke and Lindblom's indebtedness
to Popper, complicated because Chadwick, and also Wilson (1969),
embrace Popper's scientific method, yet at the same time reject disjointed
incrementalism. He might have added Hart and Gillingwater.

The fact that both proponents and opponents of disjointed incrementalism
refer to Popper approvingly raises suspicion in Camhis's mind. It also
provides him with the occasion of stating Popper's views on both piecemeal
engineering and falsification. These are useful accounts. But the question
as to the relation between falsification and disjointed incrementalism—
Camhis's central argument in this chapter—remains unanswered. Rather,
like others before him, Camhis tries to pull a trick on Popper:

> "The question which now arises is whether Popper follows his own
> methodological rules in his socio-political theories. Piecemeal social
> engineering is considered to be the only possible method and the
> corresponding doctrine the true one. But if a theory dogmatically
> claims to be true, it immediately loses its claim for a scientific status.
> A scientific hypothesis, says Popper, can never be called 'true' ... Thus,
> Popper falls short of his own standard of criticism and 'tentativeness'."
> (page 47)

Popper's answer to Lakatos, described in chapter 1, obviously applies
to Camhis: piecemeal engineering is *not* an empirical hypothesis but a
methodological proposition. Attempting to falsify it does not make sense.
To be sure, criticisms remain possible. Thus, a critic might attempt to show
that situations are conceivable in which Popper's strictures against an over-
ambitious 'holistic' approach (see chapter 5) are unwarranted. Chadwick
has been shown to hint at such situations, as does Donnison (1972) in his
critique of incrementalism:

> "Try getting the British to drive on the right of the road, incrementally.
> Could anything useful be learnt from a small, incremental piece of
> urban motorway, or a few so-called comprehensive schools added to a
> selective system of education? Some policies cannot be tried out
> incrementally on the geographical and financial scales at which we are
> obliged to operate ... If such policies have widespread implications and
> repercussions, we must do our fallible best to think and plan
> comprehensively about them." (pages 101 – 102)

None of this subtlety is found in Camhis. Rather, he takes issue with the dedication of *The Poverty of Historicism* to the victims of Nazism and Stalinism. He follows Freeman (1975) in saying that the causal influence of Marx's theories on Stalinist terror could only have been a small one and that, furthermore, this dedication should have been put in the form of a hypothesis. Both forget that Popper starts his analysis of Marx by exonerating him from any responsibilty for what happened in his name (see chapter 4). Nor does this argument shed light on Camhis's main proposition that falsification is analogous to disjointed incrementalism.

By way of concluding this chapter, Camhis reiterates this latter claim without giving any other proof than that Braybrooke and Lindblom have said so. He further gives Popper an approving clap on the back ("undoubtedly a very important figure", "educational value"; page 55), repeats the unsubstantiated allegation that his social and political philosophy is "conservative and anti-innovatory", illustrating it merely by reference to Popper's well-known enthusiasm for "our Atlantic Community", and alleges that the "... relation between Popper's politics and his scientific method cannot be reduced to a simple one-to-one correspondence" (ibid).

The problem is that Camhis confuses fallibility of human knowledge with falsificationism as the putting forward of a rule for how to obtain the most reliable universal statements about reality. Disjointed incrementalism relates to the former. But nowhere do Braybrooke and Lindblom refer to falsificationism. At first sight, of course, the link with disjointed incrementalism seems plausible. Nevertheless, the two concepts relate to different problems. Falsificationism concerns the methodological problem of how to distinguish between scientific and other statements. It is what Popper terms a demarcation criterion. Disjointed incrementalism suggests how decision-makers should proceed, given their limitations. It leads them to define decision-situations in a more limited way than any literal interpretation of rationality (Braybrooke and Lindblom's "synoptic ideal") would lead one to expect.

3.2.5 N Taylor "Planning theory and the philosophy of planning"
Whilst developing an interesting argument about the need for philosophical analysis of planning (particularly noteworthy are the references to utilitarianism) and raising relevant questions about the methodological status of my work, Taylor (1980) is quite conventional in his appreciation of Popper. It is useful, of course, to point out that the Geddesian doctrine of "Survey – Analysis – Plan" represents a crudely positivistic view of scientific method. I describe this as the object-centred view of planning. Its positivistic stance is no accident. Geddes explicitly emulates Comte (see Boardman, 1978, pages 270, 408 – 409). Also, I agree

wholeheartedly with the conclusion drawn by Taylor:

> "... that planners should not seek to gain knowledge by first doing surveys in the hope of discovering empirical proofs (as the method of 'survey‒analysis‒plan' suggests), but rather they should begin by formulating their ideas and assumptions about a given problem situation ..." (page 168).

It is the implication in the above to which one must take exception. Taylor says that ideas and assumptions should be formulated "in the form of testable hypotheses" and subjected to tests by "empirical surveys in an endeavour to show how false these hypotheses are", observing finally that "this method could also be adopted as a means of critically examining planning proposals themselves". I certainly do not wish to take issue with the critical method but, in criticising a planning proposal, one must resort to methods which are *entirely different* from those used in criticising, and perhaps falsifying, empirical hypotheses. The point has already been made with respect to Dunn and will be reiterated below when discussing the work of McConnell (1981). It will also form part of the argument of chapter 6.

3.2.6 S McConnell *Theories for Planning*

Like Taylor, McConnell (1981) identifies two areas of philosophical inquiry most relevant to planning: methodology of science and ethics. As regards the former, he takes his measure from Popper, as regards the latter from Rawls (1971). In chapter 11 I shall argue similarly that ethical theory is important for the further development of planning methodology. My main criticism of McConnell (as with Taylor and others) is that, in arguing that plans should be made testable, he is imprecise. He begins with the quite unexceptional position that

> "... even the most ethically and politically derived statements used in planning should be expressed in specific relationships to particular groups, locations and periods of time if they are to be meaningful." (page 22)

I do not take exception to the following argument either:

> "... the statements on which planning is based have to be testable in some sense—that is, there must be criteria, social and practical, against which to compare performance with expectation." (page 23)

But in the discussions which follow, he slips into talking about planning statements, rather than the statements on which they are based, giving the distinct impression that, as far as the need for "testing" them is concerned, they are the same as theories. This is confirmed later on:

> "There is ... a ... test, falsifiability, which is based on Popper's approach,
> as explained ... If planning statements are not specific in terms of what
> is meant or intended they will not be testable ... In short, unless a
> theoretical statement is expressed in such terms that it can be falsified,
> it is too imprecise to be classed as an acceptable theory." (pages 54–55)

Now, it is quite wrong to lump planning statements together with
theoretical statements and to argue that both should be made falsifiable.
Since McConnell draws on Popper, we must take "theoretical statement"
to mean hypothetical universal statement. Plans are nothing of the kind.

The point is not that they should not be as specific as possible, but that
it is misleading to say that by making them specific they are made
falsifiable. To repeat, falsification is a solution to a specific problem in
the methodology of science, that is, the distinction between scientific and
other statements.

As it stands, then, there is nothing specifically Popperian in McConnell,
although, to be sure, he gives useful accounts of Popper's teaching. There
is one exception, a short reference to Popper's "negative utilitarianism" in
a section on "Ethical theories". There, McConnell rightly observes that
"... there remains the unsurmountable problem of comparative assessments—
of suffering in this case" (page 148). He seems to forget at this point that
he himself (on page 45) has emulated the conclusion reached by Needham
and myself referred to above, namely that goals and problems "... represent
different sides of the same coin". This should have led him to reject that
"negative utilitarianism" is different anyhow.

3.2.7 P Heywood "Creativity and control in the environmental design professions"
Heywood (1982), in an article concerned with design generally, makes
global comments about the analogy between it and science. Both stem
from dissatisfaction: science from dissatisfaction with knowledge, and
design from dissatisfaction with living. Also, Heywood describes both as
making use of the capacities of the human mind for problemsolving.
Like Chadwick, Taylor, and McConnell, he concludes:

> "Both should subject their ideas to the most rigorous intellectual testing,
> so that the range of necessary physical experiments can be limited.
> Both should accept that they cannot, in the foreseeable future, achieve
> total accuracy or ultimate truth. Both should adopt an evolutionary
> view of their activities, with series of significant advances each leading
> onto the next." (pages 7–8)

Though I accept the analogy on a general level, on the more detailed
level it breaks down. This becomes evident when looking at the diagrams
which Heywood provides. There he compares hypotheses and scientific
explanations with the role which objectives play in planning. There are no

grounds for comparison between them for the simple reason that objectives are descriptions of desirable end-states and not theoretical at all.

3.2.8 E Reade, "Monitoring in planning"

Reade (1983) claims that the nub of that part of Popper's work most relevant to monitoring in planning is summed up in the phrase "policy as hypothesis". He admits that Popper does not himself use it but, on the authority of Magee (1973, page 75), he claims

> "... that the monitoring of policy is to the social sciences what laboratory experiment is to the natural sciences. When any government agency adopts any given policy, or makes any specific decision, it is in effect hypothesising that that policy or decision will have specific effects. To monitor it, therefore, and thus to investigate the extent to which it does in fact have the effects intended, is to harness the governmental process to the production of knowledge. Effective political action, therefore, not only depends upon knowledge of cause and effect, it also *produces* such knowledge." (page 227)

At this stage Reade refers to *The Open Society and its Enemies*, where Popper (1966, pages 162–163) exalts the advantages of small- over large-scale intervention because of the greater ease with which one can learn from them. Reade thinks that this puts question marks behind current practice and recommends more specific and small-scale intervention than is normally undertaken.

Reade relates all this to monitoring—"... the attempt to discover the consequences of what has been done (or attempted)" (page 224). It is based on two assumptions: (a) that it is possible to discover the consequences, (b) that the effects of policies ought to be known and freely discussed, which Reade claims is an idea very closely associated with liberalism. In chapters 6 and 11, this view will be discussed under "consequentialism". It implies

> "... a belief that the nature, and indeed the very existence, of the various activities in which government is involved must to a large extent be legitimated in terms of the effects which they produce, and that they cannot be legitimated merely by reference to arguments which suggest that these activities, or the contribution made to society by those who engage in them, are inherently desirable in themselves." (page 225)

Reade contrasts this "social science" approach to monitoring with another labelled "pragmatic" or "technocratic". The work of the 'IOR-School' (see chapter 2) is said to fall into this category. It is not my purpose to discuss this. This chapter is concerned only with the reception of Popper's work. On this, three points need to be made.

First, it is with good reason that Popper does not identify policies or plans with hypotheses. As emphasised above when discussing the work of

others making similar assertions, this is a false analogy. Plans simply lack
the formal properties of hypotheses. Admittedly, whilst implementing
them, it is possible to find out about the validity of one or more assumptions
concerning causal relations on which they are based, but then it is these
assumptions which are tested, and not the plan itself.

Second, Reade is overconcerned with learning. Surely, the main purpose
of planning is not to advance knowledge, but to take meaningful action.
Learning is a (desirable) side-effect, but not its whole point. In chapter 6,
I will argue that more is needed, therefore, than the "piecemeal engineering"
which Popper recommends, and of which Reade's suggestions for
monitoring are but a derivative: I will argue for a methodological rule for
decisionmaking and planning on *a par* with Popper's teaching concerning
the empirical sciences.

Third, it must be said that, in his zeal to distance himself from planners
and to underline the importance of the aloof position of social-science critic,
Reade forgets that planning involves applying analysis to *decisionmaking*.
The proposal in chapter 6—that rationality be regarded as a rule for
discriminating between correct and incorrect decisions (a rule fully in
accordance with the criteria as set out by Reade)—is designed to bring the
critical attitude and clarity of thought to bear on this. But, then, Reade
seems to believe planners are inherently incapable of clear thinking.

3.2.9 J Friedmann "The epistemology of social practice"
Friedmann (1977) is the only planning theorist referring to an idea from
late-Popperian philosophy of objective knowledge forming a world of its
own: "World 3". (In the area of management science however, Majone,
1980, has applied it in an interesting manner.) But Friedmann's attack on
this concept as supporting a bureaucratic and technocratic view of
planning is unwarranted: even if this was true, criticising Popper's concept
on that basis alone means declaring him guilty by association. Rather,
Popper's argument must be seen in the light of the problems in the theory
of knowledge which he attempts to solve. If knowledge is objective in
Popper's sense, forming a world apart from material things (World 1) and
subjective emotions (World 2), then so be it!

This is quite apart from the fact that Friedmann's understanding of
Popper's views on objective knowledge is limited. He seems to think that
Popper conceives of it as being objectively true. But Popper's point is
different. As soon as we part with them, the products of our minds
acquire an existence of their own. Also, in contrast to what Friedmann
assumes, Popper's World 3 does not include only scientific theories—*all*
products of the human mind are admitted.

But I am in full agreement with Friedmann that the concept of a
World 3 needs to be explored for its planning implications. In chapter 8
I shall do so.

3.3 Summary and questions arising

Other more passing references to the work of Popper might be added. Thus, Batty (1980), Eversley (1973), Wilson (1969), Rittel and Webber (1973), and Friend et al, (1974) adopt certain of his recommendations. Discussing them would not add significantly to the above.

I have shown that, in his social philosophy, Popper warns against an unthinking acceptance of central planning. His reasons include man's inability to perform this intellectual task. In the modern literature, Braybrooke and Lindblom (1963) are the first to emulate this argument.

The modern planning debate reflects concern for rendering planning scientific. Popper's view of science is referred to more often than his social philosophy. This I applaud. To be sure, Popper's arguments against central planning remain powerful, especially where they refer to man's limited intellectual capacities. But the crux is just this: their main thrust is directed against a naive (and thus dangerous) form of planning. Little can be gleaned from them as to the methodology of a modest form of planning, the need for which Popper would probably accept.

Even where I do draw on Popper's social philosophy, I emphasise elements other than those usually referred to, namely critical dualism, situational analysis and, above all, his consequentialism (see chapters 6 and 7).

The literature reveals at best a somewhat superficial acceptance of Popper's view of science. It discusses general ideas like "error elimination". At the worst, concepts with a precise meaning, like falsification, are applied inappropriately in planning. Clearly, a more thorough examination is needed of what a Popperian approach to the formulation of planning methodology really involves. Also, we must have a clear view of Popper's work. This is what I attempt to provide in chapters 4 and 5. They form the background to proposals as regards a Popperian planning methodology forming the main argument of Part 2.

Part 2

The philosophy of Sir Karl Popper and its relevance to planning methodology

Part 2 is the main part of this work. Chapter 4 gives an account of Popper's work as I came to appreciate it. Chapter 5 homes in on Popper's views on planning. As mentioned in Part 1, he participated in the classic planning debate of the 'thirties and 'forties, arguing with Hayek and others that central planning was not a scientifically sound proposition. Elsewhere in his work, he expresses views which, although not couched in terms of planning, are still relevant to planning methodology.

These two chapters form the background to the development which follows of my own Popperian approach to planning methodology. Chapter 6 forms the centrepiece. It shows that neither Popper's "piecemeal engineering", nor indeed his falsificationism, are a sufficient base for planning methodology. Rather, we must define a new demarcation criterion and a decision rule, both specially suited for the purpose of planning. They are: consequentialism (only admissible are such arguments concerning decisions as are couched in terms of their expected consequences; the term is culled from Regan, 1980, page 1, where he puts it forward as a better alternative to utilitarianism) and rationality (always take that decision which results from an evaluation of all its alternatives in the light of all their consequences).

These ideas are developed further in chapter 7 by culling building blocks from Popper's work for defining decision-situations. The same is done in chapter 8 with his late philosophy, and special attention is paid to the role of communication in planning. In chapter 9 I show that the principles of my normative planning theory developed previously are in line with Popper's thinking.

A personal view of Popperian philosophy

Some excellent introductions to Popper's work exist. The slim volume by
Magee (1973) rightly enjoys popularity. Recently, Parekh (1982) has
succeeded in giving an even briefer account of the interrelationships
between Popperian methodology of science and social philosophy. I do
not aim to better these accounts. This chapter merely contains my
personal understanding of Popper's work as it developed in conjunction
with planning methodological concerns.

My sympathy with Popper's work results from a long-standing concern
for bringing reason and tolerance to bear on the conduct of our affairs.

The origin of Popper's work stems from early suspicions about the claims
of Marxist policies to be scientifically based. This has turned Popper's
attention to the theory of science. His *The Logic of Scientific Discovery*
criticises inductivism. Popper argues that, instead of generalising from the
facts, one should seek out falsifying instances of general statements. This
work will be discussed first. The next criticises 'historicism', arguing that
the social sciences should aim at scientifically predicting the development
of mankind. Popper's second social philosophical work applies this
critique to Plato, Hegel, and Marx. His late philosophy develops themes
of earlier books, amongst them a theory of problemsolving, an evolutionary
theory of knowledge, and the notion of "World 3".

4.1 My approach to Popper

A few hints will make clear that my reasons for emulating Popper go
further than our common Viennese background. They include a preference
for rationalism as a way of going about human affairs.

Many of those visiting my parent's home in the late 1950s had spent
World War II abroad. They provided a wider perspective than the
somewhat stultified social and political outlook of the Vienna of the time.
I was impressed by conversations turning on the absence, in the Austrian
postwar political spectrum, of any genuinely liberal party, which I associated
with reason and tolerance. At the same time, many of my peers were
apolitical, or even inclined towards the extreme right.

None of this played a part in my studying architecture. In specialising
in planning, I did hope though to be able to find an intellectually sound
approach to an area of great practical concern.

Alas, I was to be disappointed. As did many other planners, I turned
to the social sciences for intellectual nourishment. Longing to reach out
beyond the bounds of my situation, I went to study them abroad. The
biographies of many European academics bear evidence of the dividends
that have accrued to bursaries then available for this purpose, mostly for
study in the United States. It was England in my case.

Maurice Broady's seminars at the University of Southampton were a revelation. We read Mannheim's *Man and Society in an Age of Reconstruction* (1940), Popper's critique of it in Part 3 of *The Poverty of Historicism* (1961), Braybrooke and Lindblom's *A Strategy of Decision* (1963), and Friedmann's article on "Planning as a vocation" (1966/67). They all evolved around the very questions which had driven me away from architecture: the meaning of a rational—and tolerant—conduct of human affairs.

At the time, Mannheim and Friedmann fascinated me more than Popper, and my subsequent teaching and research at the Oxford Polytechnic developed along their lines. As regards the critique of planning, I mostly referred to Lindblom.

Acquaintance with Popper's methodology of science resulted from discussions with one of the last generation of Popper's students at the London School of Economics, Steve Chait. Needham's article referred to in chapter 3 further raised my awareness of Popper's work. Its implications for planning theory were central to debates (referred to in the Acknowledgements) in the wake of publication of *Planning Theory*. By that time, I had read most of it together with Magee's appreciative account. Soon I was to read Popper's Autobiography (1974a), and my sympathy grew. This chapter, then, gives my view of Popper's work resulting from these pursuits.

4.2 The origin of Popper's work

There is a 'Popper-legend' which he tries to dispel in his Autobiography: that he has been a member of the Vienna Circle and that he is a positivist. I shall discuss both below. But there is a further element in this legend to which he himself has contributed. This is that his main interest, as evidenced in his *Logik der Forschung* (1935; published in English as late as 1959 under *The Logic of Scientific Discovery*) is in the methods of the natural sciences and that his social and political philosophy is of the nature of an afterthought. (See Popper, 1966, volume 1, page 2; 1974a, page 69)

His Autobiography leaves room for another interpretation giving primacy to his social and political concerns. (See also the "Historical Note" in Popper, 1966.) Under hothouse conditions in Vienna, when revolution was imminent during and after the Great War, he had become a Communist. Shortly before his seventeenth birthday, young Socialists, instigated by the Communists, had tried to free other Communists from police custody and were shot. The young Popper was shocked by the belief, which he had espoused himself, "... that although the revolution may claim some victims, capitalism is claiming more victims than the whole socialist revolution ..." (1974a, page 25). He began to doubt "... whether such a calculation could ever be supported by 'science'" (ibid), as it was claimed for it.

This experience led him to become sceptical concerning knowledge generally, eventually leading to his philosophy of science as laid down in

The Logic of Scientific Discovery. He concluded that science can provide no unambiguous base for politics. Consequently, the first of his two works on social philosophy, *The Poverty of Historicism*, is dedicated as follows:

> "In memory of the countless men and women of all creeds or nations or races who fell victims to the Fascist and Communist belief in Inexorable Laws of Historical Destiny."

Most see this as a reference to the nightmarish events of World War II when *The Poverty of Historicism* was published. But there is a continuity of concern reaching back to that formative event in his youth.

4.3 *The Logic of Scientific Discovery*

His Autobiography describes the further development of Popper's thinking. The Vienna Circle of eminent scientists and philosophers mentioned above argued at the time that only those statements deserved to be called scientific which could be verified by observations and that, except for statements expressing logical relations (so called analytical statements), these alone were meaningful.

Popper became uneasy when he found that both Marxism and Freud's theories were supported by *many* observations.   Einstein though, presenting his theory of relativity, had said that, as soon as a crucial experiment contradicted it, he would recant his theory. (The crucial experiment involved observations of the influence of gravity on light and necessitated the mounting of an expedition in 1919 to observe a complete eclipse of the sun. It did *not* contradict Einstein.)

This aroused Popper's suspicion as regards verification. It involves induction, that is the derivation of general propositions from particular observations. Popper's now famous argument is that this is impossible, logically speaking. We can never exclude the possibility of future observations contradicting such conclusions. Thus, the truth of general propositions can *never* be established conclusively. But their falsity *can* be established. If one swan is ever known to be black, and not white, then the proposition: 'All swans are white' is false, no matter how many white ones fly about.

So, Popper proposed a different solution to the 'demarcation problem'. General propositions about reality, or hypotheses, are scientific if, and only if, they lend themselves to falsification. In this way, Popper claims to have "killed logical positivism", which is the name under which the philosophy of the Vienna Circle goes (see 1974a, pages 69–71).

There is another gulf separating him from logical positivists, who abhor statements which cannot be verified as metaphysical. Popper has always maintained that there are genuine philosophical problems which cannot be resolved by reference to observations. An example which bewildered Parmenides is this: If something changes, then clearly it becomes something different from what it was before. Yet equally clearly, that something must also remain the same, otherwise we could not talk about "it" changing. So how can one give a coherent account of change? Solving this problem involves philosophical argument, not empirical analysis.

It must have hurt Popper to be labelled a 'positivist' during the positivistic dispute in German sociology (Adorno et al, 1976). But during that dispute the term has acquired a different meaning, referring to everything despicable about science, including the application of the methods of the natural to the social sciences.

In a way, Popper does just this in his two works on social and political philosophy, although he also recognises differences between them. Before turning to them, some further arguments of *The Logic of Scientific Discovery* need to be presented. One concerns the type of problem which any methodology should address. Reference to this has already been made in the course of identifying the core argument of *Planning Theory* as being methodological. The reader will remember the distinction between a "logic of discovery" and a "logic of justification", and that Popper is concerned only with the latter.

Another has to do with Popper's rejection of logical positivism. According to the latter, the only things which are real are sense impressions. Ultimately, since sense impressions are inside ourselves, this leads to the extreme view that nothing exists outside: what is called solipsism. Popper restores commonsense realism as a necessary *assumption* underlying human conduct. He also adopts a theory of absolute truth formulated by Tarski: Truth is nothing else but being in complete accord with reality.

But how can we attain truth, given that our hypotheses can never be conclusively verified? Popper's answer is simple: we can *not*. But by relentlessly falsifying hypotheses, we may approximate truth in asymptotic fashion. This is similar to what is often said about planning: the pursuit of an ideal, such as rational planning, results in learning. I shall develop this point further in chapter 6.

Critics retort that, in falsifying hypotheses, Popper *is* referring to observations as the last court of appeal, just as logical positivists do. Popper's answer is that there are no observations of "reality as it is". It is possible to disagree about the facts. Thus, whether an experiment refutes a hypothesis may be open to doubt. There may have been an error of measurement; or some unknown variable has been interfering with the experimental setup. Popper describes this as the problem of formulating *basic statements*.

Uncertainty about basic statements notwithstanding, Popper says that scientists can mostly agree upon them. He compares this with judicial procedures, where the verdict on what has happened involves quite different considerations from those in passing judgement. It is a matter of taking a decision:

> "By its decision, the jury accepts, by agreement, a statement about a
> factual occurence—a basic statement as it were. The significance of this
> decision lies in the fact that from it, together with the universal statement
> of the system (of criminal law) certain consequences can be deduced.
> In other words, the decision forms the basis for the application of the
> system; the verdict plays the part of a 'true statement of fact'. But it is
> clear that the statement need not be true merely because the jury has
> accepted it. This fact is acknowledged in the rule allowing a verdict to
> be quashed or revised." (Popper, 1959, pages 109–110)

The analogy with the verdict of the jury will figure again in chapter 6,
where it will be extended to definitions of decision situations. They are
also of the nature of basic statements and subject to agreement.

A page further on Popper uses another example which, since coming to
The Netherlands with its poor soil conditions, has its specific charm for me:

> "The empirical basis of objective science has thus nothing 'absolute'
> about it. Science does not rest upon solid bedrock. The bold structure
> of its theories rises, as it were, above a swamp. It is like a building
> erected on piles. The piles are driven down from above into the
> swamp, but not down to any natural or 'given' base; and if we stop
> driving the piles deeper, it is not because we have reached firm ground.
> We simply stop when we are satisfied that the piles are firm enough to
> carry the structure, at least for the time being." (Popper, 1959, page 111)

So, both theories (hypotheses) and basic statements *might* be wrong. If
they *contradict* each other, they cannot *both* be right. It all comes down
to the principle of consistency: you cannot believe that anything exists,
whilst at the same time believing that a law prevails which says that it
does not do so. Whether you decide to change your belief in what you
think you observe, or in the validity of the law, is a separate matter. In this
way, Popper's methodology of science makes do without the—erroneous—
assumption of certainty of human knowledge, be it of facts or laws.

To summarise Popper's view on falsification, he says empirical science
is after truth, and nothing but the truth. Truth is simply correspondence
between propositions and the facts. The awareness of our inability to
obtain truth should not deter us from searching for it. The way of doing
so is not the path of verificationism but of falsificationism. Falsifiability
distinguishes scientific statements from others. By trying to falsify our
hypotheses, we approach truth asymptotically. Trying to verify hypotheses
simply leads us away from truth towards formulating more and more
empty statements. (Statements which are empty are always true!)

Falsification is thus a *demarcation criterion*. But it does not help us in
deciding between a number of falsifiable hypotheses. But criteria of
choice between scientific theories—each of them falsifiable as such theories

should be—are also to be found in Popper's work: theories which have withstood *more rigorous tests* should be preferred; theories which are *easier to falsify*—for which their authors have stuck their necks out more— are equally preferable. Popper also refers to the truth content of theoretical statement: *the more a theory forbids*—the more falsifying instances there are—the more we may trust that theory. Thus, next to the demarcation criterion, Popper's methodology of the empirical sciences also offers a *decision rule for choosing between hypotheses.* Though clearly related to it, this aspect of his view of science is less well known than falsification.

The Logic of Scientific Discovery does not address planning. *The Poverty of Historicism* and *The Open Society and its Enemies* do, drawing parallels with Popper's views on science. As we shall see, these works include a powerful condemnation of what we presently describe as blueprint planning. They are closely related, and formed what Popper describes as his "war effort" in his Autobiography (see 1974a, page 91).

After the general outline of these works below, I shall go into more detail in chapter 5 as regards Popper's views on planning—he mostly talks about "engineering"—contained mainly in Part 3 of *The Poverty of Historicism.*

4.4 *The Poverty of Historicism*
In this book, Popper (1961) has "... tried hard to present historicism as a well-considered and close-knit philosophy" (page 3). Parts 1 and 2 deal with its "anti-naturalistic" and "pro-naturalistic" doctrines. They are then demolished in Parts 3 and 4. In so doing, Popper gives his views on the social sciences, social philosophy and practice, including his views on planning.

Why historicism, and why these various doctrines? Historicism is a view concerning the social sciences, namely

> "... that historical prediction is their principal aim, and ... that this aim is attainable by discovering the 'rhythms' or the 'patterns', the 'laws' or the 'trends' that underlie the evolution of history." (page 3)

The reason for criticising it is that it is dangerous: historicism exercises a spell, even on well-intentioned people. It makes them accept horrible crimes and sacrifices as inevitable, simply because, supposedly, their necessity is scientifically proven. As we have seen, as a young man, Popper has been under the spell himself. Thus, when there was the danger of historicism prevailing in World War II, he set out to fight it with the means at his disposal: argument.

The distinction between pronaturalistic and antinaturalistic doctrines relates to Hayek's concept of "scientism". It was at one of Hayek's seminars that the paper from which this book originated was given. In fact, Popper tacitly criticised "scientism" as representing a misguided effort to copy the methods of the natural sciences in social affairs (what is currently called with a misleading term "positivism").

So, Popper discusses this problem in terms of an anti' and pronaturalistic doctrine. The former says that the study of society (exemplified in *The Poverty of Historicism* by the study of history) should develop its own methods, the latter that it should rather emulate the example of the natural sciences. In these terms, Hayek is an antinaturalist.

Popper seems uninterested in this issue as such. He merely points out that historicism inadvertently combines both pro' and antinaturalistic doctrines and shows a lack of understanding of what scientific method really is. His criticism of Hayek—introduced in passing as a modification of the concept of scientism—is therefore that, really, he could not have meant the imitation of science proper, but of "... *what certain people mistake* for the method and language of science" (page 105, note 1). Perhaps it is also out of respect for Hayek that Popper never returns to the issue of pro' versus antinaturalism, using the two concepts as vehicles for demolishing historicism and for expounding his own views instead.

I shall now describe Popper's notion of historicism. From antinaturalism, it draws the conviction "... that some of the characteristic methods of physics cannot be applied to the social sciences, owing to the profound differences ..." (page 5). The reason is that sociological laws "... differ in different places and periods" (ibid). Immutable regularities as are said to exist in the physical world just do not prevail. Based on this, Popper parades an array of arguments against applying the methods of the natural sciences in the social realm, which make the reader wonder what the positivistic dispute might have added. Special emphasis is given to holism, the doctrine that social entities are "more than the sum of their parts", and to intuitive understanding as the appropriate methods of the social sciences. Historicism often involves both.

The pronaturalistic doctrines of historicism view the social sciences as being similar to physics. Therefore, they should be able to identify historical laws, or trends, and to make forecasts possible, as in astronomy, only less precise.

How do historicists reconcile this quest for historical laws with their belief that there can be no generalisations as between places and historic periods? They say the only conceivable social laws are those explaining the transition from one period to the next. These do not require to assume regularities as between periods. The practical purpose of "laws of historical development" is this:

"If the attempt to furnish us with political foresight of scientific validity were to succeed, then sociology would prove to be of the greatest value to politicians, especially to those whose vision extends beyond the exigencies of the present, to politicians with a sense of historical destiny." (page 42)

According to historicists, this is indeed what is needed. At the same time, they have no regard for rational planning:

"Any social science which does not teach the impossibility of rational social construction is entirely blind to the most important facts of social life, and must overlook the only social laws of real validity and of real importance." (page 48)

Historicism does not condemn us to inactivity though. It rather channels our activism:

"Only such plans as fit in with the main current of history can be effective ... Social midwifery is the only wholly reasonable activity open to us, the only activity that can be based on scientific foresight." (page 49)

This is what makes historicism into such a peculiar philosophy of action. He who has scientific insight cannot err, but he has *no choice either.* Paraphrasing Marx saying philosophers should stop interpreting the world and get down to changing it, Popper comments:

"The historicist can only interpret social development and aid it in various ways; his point, however, is that nobody can change it." (page 52)

Popper goes on to the antinaturalistic doctrines of historicism. Here his approach is more indirect but yields rich results for our central concern, planning methodology. First he states his own views as regards the successful method of "piecemeal technology" or "piecemeal engineering". It is what Popper is most famous for in planning circles. Since I shall discuss it in chapters 5 and 6, I concentrate on criticisms of historicism advanced thereafter.

Historicists claim that human development must be studied as a whole (holism). But they overlook that "... 'wholes' ... can never be the object of scientific inquiry" (page 74). Also, the pronaturalistic doctrines of historicism are simply based on misunderstanding of the methods of the natural sciences. A hypothesis concerning human development "as a whole" can never be of the nature of a law because it is not a universal statement. Rather, it is a singular statement about a unique set of events:

"... any law ... must be tested by new instances before it can be taken seriously by science. But we cannot hope to test a universal hypothesis ... if we are confined to the observation of one unique process. Nor can the observation of one unique process help us to foresee its future development." (page 109)

For this reason, history is simply *not* a theoretical science. Like applied scientists, historians rather use universal laws taken from other sciences in explaining singular historical events. (Planners do the same, but for situations with a future dimension; see chapter 7.)

4.5 *The Open Society and its Enemies*
In this book Popper (1966) shows

"... that this civilization has not yet fully recovered from the shock of its birth—the transition from the tribal or 'closed society', with its submission to magical force, to the 'open society' which sets free critical powers of man ..."

[Popper] "... thereby tries to contribute to our understanding of totalitarianism, and of the significance of the perennial fight against it." (volume 1, page 1)

In so doing, he

"... tries to clear away some of the obstacles impeding a rational approach to the problems of social reconstruction ... by criticizing those social philosophies which are responsible for the widespread prejudice against the possibility of democratic reform." (pages 1–2)

Popper relates this to his misgivings about historicism and Utopianism, stressing instead our responsibility for our decisions:

"... we may become the makers of our fate when we have ceased to pose as its prophets." (page 4)

He singles out for criticism three advocates of a 'closed society': Plato (in volume 1) and Hegel and Marx (in volume 2). Much has been written about Popper's interpretations. My interest here is only with their implications for planning methodology. But, we cannot do entirely without an account of the argument because, as in *The Poverty of Historicism*, Popper makes a habit of contrasting his own views with those he criticises as he goes along. For instance, he does so when discussing Plato's historicism. Plato had performed a keen sociological analysis of ancient Greek tribal society and of the forces of change towards a more open, democratic society. He also believed that it was possible to reverse this trend, opposed as it was to the aristocratic society of his forefathers. Thus, Plato combined historicism with a form of (Utopian, see below) social engineering: his ends derived from historicist argument, but he was perfectly willing to use his knowledge concerning human institutions to achieve them. He gave much attention also to how the institutions of his ideal state, including education and human breeding, could be so designed as to arrest change, once these ends had been achieved.

Popper says that Plato was a holist, entertaining an "organic theory of the state" (page 81) subordinating the individual to the community. This leads Popper into an analysis of the relationship between empirical knowledge and the setting of norms which, as we shall see, is relevant for planning methodology. It is this: in a 'closed society', laws and customs are seen as immutable, much as the regularities of nature are. Popper calls this monism. His own view he describes as critical dualism. He relates this to the breakdown of the closed society. Comparisons between different societies had revealed to the ancient Greeks that 'nature' and 'society' were different (page 60) and that norms were a matter of choice and not of divine origin. This Plato feared, for he was opposed to people choosing freely. Nowadays we would describe his programme as totalitarian.

How could this be with a philosopher whose name is linked to the analysis of justice? But justice, in Plato's terms, prevails "... if the ruler rules, if the worker works, and if the slave slaves" (page 90), all in accordance with the essence of his ideal state. Popper contrasts this with the prevailing humanitarian theory of justice in Athens aiming to eliminate privileges, uphold individualism, and limit the role of the state to that of protector of the freedom of its citizens.

Popper also discusses Plato's famous claim that the philosophers should be king, pointing out that this meant the rule of learnedness concerning the "divine world of Forms and Ideas" (page 145):

"Philosophic natures are lovers of that kind of learning which reveals to them a reality that exists for ever and is not harassed by generation and degeneration. It does not seem that Plato's treatment of wisdom can carry him beyond the ideal of arresting change." (page 146)

Linking his analysis of Plato with his ideas from *The Poverty of Historicism*, Popper draws a distinction between various forms of historicism, one radical (represented by Marx) and one less radical (represented by Plato). The first says "... that we cannot alter the course of history ..." (page 157), the second sees possibilities for human interference, if only on a massive scale, requiring amongst other things centralised rule. It demands Utopian engineering (for details see chapter 5), dealing with "... society as a whole, leaving no stone unturned ..." (page 164). Plato's radicalism in this matter has to do with his aestheticism, his dreams of perfection:

"Plato was an artist; and like many of the best artists, he tried to visualize a model, the 'divine original' of his work, and to 'copy' it faithfully ... Politics, to Plato, is the Royal Art ... It is an art of composition, like music, painting, or architecture. The Platonic politician composes cities, for beauty's sake.

"But here I must protest. I do not believe that human lives may be made the means of satisfying an artist's desire for self-expression. We must demand, rather, that every man should be given, if he wishes, the right to model his life himself, as far as this does not interfere too much with others." (page 165)

Popper demonstrates the extent to which Plato was willing to 'clean the canvass' to create something more to his liking. But the political artist places himself outside the social world

"... in order to lever it off its hinges. But such a place does not exist; and the social world must continue to function during any reconstruction.

This is the simple reason why we must reform its institutions little by little, until we have more experience in social engineering." (page 167)

Volume 2 begins with analysing Aristotelian roots of Hegelianism before turning to Hegel himself. Popper has no respect for him at all, but this part has no bearing on planning methodology. For Marx, however, Popper shows a great deal of sympathy. He begins by exonerating Marx from any responsibility whatsoever for the totalitarianism of Soviet Russia; his is a

"... purely historical theory, a theory which aims at predicting the future course of economic and power-political developments and especially of revolutions. As such, it certainly did not furnish the basis of the policy of the Russian Communist Party ... The vast economic researches of Marx did not even touch the problem of a constructive economic policy, for example, economic planning." (volume 2, pages 82-83)

Popper treats Marxism as a method and criticises it similarly to historicism. He also claims that Marx's concept of science (which underlies his historicism) is thoroughly outdated:

"Scientific method cannot be said to favour the adoption of strict determinism. Science can be rigidly scientific without this assumption. Marx, of course, cannot be blamed for having held the opposite view, since the best scientists of his day did the same." (page 85)

Comparing Marx with John Stuart Mill allows Popper to give his views on the latter's psychologism, that is, the view that social laws must be reduced to psychological laws. He defends Marx's advocacy of the autonomy of sociology against Mill. But Mill's individualism he applauds. In so doing, he gives his own view on institutions being the largely unintended by-products of human actions, as well as on situational logic (see chapters 5 and 7). Marx's "economic historicism" meets with disapproval. It is said to overrate the influence of economic conditions. His concept of class may be seen as a hypothesis, but one that has been falsified. Marx's theory of the state is essentialist, that is, aimed at answering the question of "what is the state?" Such questions can never be answered conclusively. Furthermore, Marx's view that the state is a reflection of economic reality condemns politics to impotence.

But Popper's quarrels with Marx do not concern his revulsion with unrestrained capitalism. Popper professes himself to be an advocate of interventionism (see chapter 5).

Having criticised Marx's method, Popper shows that many of his substantive propositions have been falsified by events. In passing, he explains his attitude towards violence, the use of which

"... is justified only under a tyranny and ... should have only one aim, that is, to bring about a state of affairs which makes reform without violence possible." (page 151)

The last section on Marx deals with his ethics. Implicit in the criticism of capitalism is an ethics of, and a faith in, the open society. But this is counteracted by Marx's historicism. From this, he is said to have concluded that

"... reason can have no part in bringing about a more reasonable world." (page 202)

This leads to what Popper calls Marx's historicist moral theory. It holds that ethical ideas reflect class positions, leading to relativism (which Popper abhors). The only decisions which do not are those based on detached (Marxist) analysis of historic development. They are not moral but scientific. In this way, the historicist moral theory becomes a weapon for attacking others whilst making Marx's own position unassailable. Even if we assume that historic developments *can* be analysed as Marx does, this moral theory must be criticised. It is based on the principle that 'coming might is right'. Even when developments seem inevitable, one can morally reject them, because Popper maintains that moral judgement is logically independent from factual judgement.

That our thoughts are determined by our social positions—what Popper calls Marx's sociologism and which he castigates in the more recent sociology of knowledge—can be criticised on other grounds as well. Sociologism is not only opposed to a rational approach to human affairs (see above), it also misunderstands scientific method and the nature of objectivity. The latter does not—indeed must not—depend on individuals (not even on Mannheim's "freely poised intelligentsia"; see Mannheim, 1940) but on the institution of criticism:

"That our minds, our views, are in a way a product of 'society' is trivially true. The most important part of our environment is its social part; thought, in particular, is very largely dependent on social intercourse; ... But it simply cannot be denied that we can examine thoughts, that we can criticize. Thus, we can change and improve our physical environment according to our changed, improved thoughts. And the same is true of our social environment." (page 209)

Here comes Popper's definition of rationalism (already noted in chapter 1) as the attitude of saying:

"I may be wrong and you may be right, and by an effort we may get nearer to the truth." (page 225)

As with science, the character of rationalism is social (later modified to "inter-personal", see page 226) and egalitarian:

"We must recognize everybody with whom we communicate as a potential source of argument." (page 225)

True rationalism recognises though that we must not expect too much from reason. In this respect, Popper distinguishes between *uncritical* and *critical* rationalism. The first says that one should never accept any statement except when supported by argument. Such a view is logically untenable because it itself cannot be based on argument. All argument must begin with assumptions, therefore. The rationalist attitude is no exception. Thus, critical rationalism "... recognises that the fundamental rationalist attitude results from an (at least tentative) act of faith—from faith in reason." (page 231)

This is a moral decision. It can be taken by considering its consequences. Irrationalism ultimately leads to inequality and inhumane attitudes; rationalism to equality and humanism. Here, Popper gives his reasons referred to in chapter 1 for opting for rationalism.

The final chapter discusses the question "Has history any meaning?". It repeats the argument from *The Poverty of Historicism* that descriptions, including historical descriptions, must be selective. It also compares history with the theoretical sciences, exploring the "covering law" model of explanation on the way. The "logic of the situation" is compared with scientific hypotheses. There can be various interpretations, each with its own logic, of historic situations, Popper concludes. Thus, history as such has no meaning, but we can give it meaning. This is in line with Popper's critical dualism, about which more in chapter 5.

4.6 Popper's late philosophy

Popper has written many addenda and explanatory notes to his works in later years. Much of his subsequent work—*Conjectures and Refutations* (1963) and *Objective Knowledge* (1973, 1st edition 1972)—is a commentary on, and an elaboration of, earlier views. Of relevance to planning methodology are: his theory of problemsolving; his evolutionary theory of knowledge and the role of language therein; his notion of "World 3" as the world of objective knowledge.

The theory of problemsolving builds on *The Logic of Scientific Discovery*. The 'Preface to the first English edition' written in 1958 already presents falsification as but an instance of the critical method:

"... I am quite ready to admit that there is a method which might be described as 'the one method of philosophy'. But it is not characteristic of philosophy alone; it is, rather, the one method of all *rational discussion*, and therefore of the natural sciences as well as of philosophy. The method I have in mind is that of stating one's problem clearly and of examining its various proposed solutions *critically*.

"I have italicized the words 'rational discussion' and 'critically' in order to stress that I equate the rational attitude and the critical attitude." (Popper, 1959, page 16)

This theory of problemsolving underlying all rational discourse is encapsulated in the title *Conjectures and Refutations*. The terms stand for tentative solutions to problems and for success in eliminating them through criticism. Popper explains it as follows:

"... every rational theory, no matter whether scientific of philosophical, is rational in so far as it tries to solve certain problems. A theory is comprehensible and reasonable only in its relation to a given problem situation, and it can be rationally discussed only by discussing this relation.

"Now if we look upon a theory as a proposed solution to a set of problems, then the theory immediately lends itself to critical discussion ... For we can now ask questions such as, Does it solve the problem? Does it solve it better than other theories? ..." (Popper, 1963, page 199)

The fullest exposition is to be found in *Objective Knowledge* (1973):

"The activity can be represented by a general schema of problem-solving by the method of imaginative conjectures and criticism ..."

"The schema (in its simplest form) is this

   P1 → TT → EE → P2

Here P1 is the problem from which we start, TT (the tentative theory) is the imaginative conjectural solution ... EE ('error elimination') consists of a severe critical examination of our conjecture ... and, if we have at this early stage more than one conjecture at our disposal, it will consist of a critical discussion and comparative evaluation of the competing conjectures. P2 is the problem situation as it emerges from our first critical attempt to solve our problems. It leads up to our second attempt (*and so on*)." (page 164)

According to Popper's evolutionary theory of knowledge, all living organisms can be seen as problemsolvers. Since Darwin, evolution is thought to result from what is commonly described as the "survival of the fittest". The critique of hypothetical solutions—conjectures—is but its continuation in the realm of knowledge. Even organisms embody solutions to problems. Their elimination is equivalent to their refutation—hence "evolutionary" theory of knowledge.

This sheds light also on whether there are objective facts, or observational (as against theoretical) statements, as logical positivists would have it. As we know, Popper rejected this in *The Logic of Scientific Discovery* (1959). He now says that, what our sense organs perceive is influenced by their make-up embodying successful (thus far not eliminated) theories of our evolutionary past. This is another sense in which we may understand Popper's dictum: facts are theory-impregnated.

An interesting part of his evolutionary theory is its application to humans. Here, he dwells on the role of language. It has various functions of which the argumentative one is the most important:

"The tremendous biological advance of the invention of a descriptive and argumentative language can now be seen more precisely than before: the linguistic formulation of theories allows us to criticize and to eliminate them without eliminating the race which carries them. This is the first achievement. The second achievement is the development of a conscious and systematic attitude of criticism towards our theories. With this begins the method of science ..." (Popper, 1973, page 70).

The above leads to Popper's notion of a "World 3" of objective knowledge. The meaning of 'objective' (which escaped Friedmann; see chapter 3) is a subject broached in the Foreword of *Objective Knowledge*:

"The essays in this book break with a tradition that can be traced to Aristotle—the tradition of the common sense theory of knowledge as a subjectivist blunder. This blunder has dominated Western philosophy. I have made an attempt to eradicate it, and to replace it by an objective theory of essentially conjectural knowledge." (Page VII; the "blunder" will be explained below.)

Popper's theory rests on two propositions: that knowledge is objective and hypothetical. The second leads to falsificationism. It is with the first that we are concerned here.

In describing knowledge as objective, Popper does not, of course, mean to say that it is certain. This would run foul of his view of knowledge as fallible. But, as soon as we have parted with the products of our thoughts, they acquire an existence of their own. The most extensive discussion is to be found in the book written jointly with Eccles, *The Self and its Brain*. There, Popper asks when we would regard something as *real*. His answer is:

"... that the entities which we conjecture to be real should be able to exert a causal effect upon the *prima facie* real things; that is, upon material things of an ordinary size ..." (Popper and Eccles, 1977, page 9).

Thus, concepts like atom, force, force field etc

"... may be described as highly abstract theoretical entities; yet as they interact in a direct or indirect way with ordinary material things, we accept them as real ..." (page 10).

Of course, the hypothetical character of knowledge remains. So, our view of what is real can change:

"... having learned about physical forces, events, and processes, we may discover that material things, especially solids, are to be interpreted as very special physical processes, in which molecular forces play a dominant role ..." (ibid).

This is where his concept of a "World 3" comes in:

"First, there is the physical world—the universe of physical entities—...;
this I will call 'World 1'. Second, there is the world of mental states; ...
this I will call 'World 2'. But there is also a third such world, the world
of the contents of thought, and, indeed, of the products of the human
mind; this I will call 'World 3' ..." (page 38).

World-3 objects are: stories, explanatory myths, tools, scientific theories
(whether true or false), scientific problems, social institutions, and works
of art. Many of these exist in the form of material (World 1) objects. But
what is significant is their content. To this, Popper ascribes an existence
of its own:

"One of my main theses is that World 3-objects can be real ... not only
in their World 1 materializations ... but also in their World 3-aspects.
As World 3-objects, they may induce men to produce other World 3-
objects and, thereby, to act on World 1; and interaction with World 1—
even indirect interaction—I regard as a decisive argument for calling a
thing real". (page 40)

With his worlds, Popper attacks the "*common sense theory of knowledge*".
Knowledge does not require the assumption of a knowing subject, as this
theory—the subjectivist blunder mentioned above—asserts. Rather,
knowledge is a collective product. This applies to scientific knowledge in
particular. One need only think of the role ascribed by Popper to the
community of scientists. It is with respect to scientific knowledge that the
preconditions of refining knowledge—of attaining, as Popper would have
it, verisimilitude—are particularly good. What is meant is, of course, the
falsification principle which takes us back to the hypothetical character
of knowledge. Popper therefore ascribes a prominent role to scientific
knowledge (as laid down in accessible form: books, articles, etc.) in
'World 3'.

4.7 Conclusions
There is a human concern at the heart of Popper's philosophy: the
concern for suffering, for the tragedy of human sacrifices. This has given
rise to his views of what should, and what should not, be expected of
science, and how we should, and should not, approach human conduct
generally. The scepticism aroused in his youth prevails throughout his
work, together with his humanism—particularly evident where he stresses
our responsibility for our fate—which we cannot eschew by hiding behind
laws of historical destiny. The same humanism is evident in his late
philosophy, especially his evolutionary theory of knowledge and the role
of language therein.

The next chapter rounds off this presentation of Popperian philosophy
by dealing specifically with his views on planning.

Popper's views on planning

This chapter is intended to convey an understanding of Popper's views on planning. Best known in planning circles is his *piecemeal engineering*, the first topic of this chapter. It is not often appreciated that one may also derive a philosophy of planning, in the sense of the self-guidance of man, from Popper's work. This is the second topic. The third is a thorny one in planning methodology: the relationship between ends and means. Popper's 'critical dualism' can illuminate it. The chapter ends with a paragraph on the "logic of the situation".

5.1 Piecemeal engineering

Having introduced the topic of 'engineering' (his equivalent of planning) in Part 2 of *The Poverty of Historicism* (1961) Popper returns to it in his critique of historicism. Much of Part 3 ("Criticisms of the anti-naturalistic doctrines") and some of Part 4 ("Criticisms of the pro-naturalistic doctrines") is taken up by discussions of what we would now call blueprint planning and the process approach. (See Faludi, 1984, pages 131–149.)

Popper presents his case by first describing what he sees as the successful method of "piecemeal technology". By way of contrast, he shows historicism to be a poor method. Now, 'piecemeal' is not only the opposite of the 'social blueprints' of collectivist planners. It also denotes acceptance of 'piecemeal tinkering', combined with criticism, as *the* way of achieving practical results. It is in this context that Popper introduces his doctrine developed in *The Logic of Scientific Discovery* (1959, pages 68–69), of the use of natural laws in their technological form:

> "... every natural law can be expressed by asserting that *such and such a thing cannot happen*: ... 'you can't carry water in a sieve' ... This way of formulating natural laws is one which makes their technological significance obvious and it may therefore be called the 'technological form' of a natural law." (1961, page 61)

"Piecemeal social engineering" stands simply for the utilisation of available knowledge for the realisation of certain aims. The latter are:

> "... beyond the province of technology. (All that technology may say about ends is whether or not they are compatible with each other or realizable.) In this it [piecemeal engineering] differs from historicism, which regards the ends of human activities as dependent on historical forces and so within its province." (page 64)

This "technological form" of empirical laws will be discussed again in chapter 7.

One is reminded of the charge levelled by Habermas against Popper and his like that their rationality is limited only to means and leaves the

ends of action out of consideration. This issue is most important for
planning, relating as it does to the respective roles and responsibilities of
planners and politicians. It is not discussed here, for the simple reason
that Popper does not discuss it in *The Poverty of Historicism*, but rather in
The Open Society and its Enemies when expounding the historicist moral
theory. In *The Poverty of Historicism* Popper goes on to develop the
method of piecemeal social engineering, or planning:

> "The characteristic approach of the piecemeal engineer is this. Even
> though he may perhaps cherish some ideas which concern society 'as a
> whole' ... he does not believe in the method of re-designing it as a whole.
> Whatever his ends, he tries to achieve them by small adjustments and
> re-adjustments which can be continually improved upon." (page 66)

This is the opposite of what Popper calls Utopian engineering,
Utopianism, or holistic engineering, all of which relate to historicism.
Indeed, criticisms of Utopian engineering are the same as those of
historicism. It

> "... aims at remodelling the 'whole of society' in accordance with a
> definite plan or blueprint; it aims at 'seizing the key positions' and at
> extending the power of the state ... until the state becomes nearly
> identical with society ..." (page 67).

The reference here is to Mannheim (1940), who draws the opposite
conclusion from the rise of Fascism in Central Europe: that there is a
need for overall planning in democracies. Popper's argument is not
against the scope of such planning, however. Contrary to what some
planning authors, discussed in chapter 3, think (and what the folklore says
about Popper's 'piecemeal engineering'), the difference between piecemeal
and Utopian engineering is not a matter of scope but of method. The
Utopian rejects a careful, critical, step-by-step approach as being too timid
and as not effective, preferring an holistic approach instead. If we take
account of the state of knowledge about the actual working of centralised
planning at the time, this analysis is striking. The ambition of the holists,
Popper says, is in stark contrast with their practice:

> "... the holistic method turns out to be impossible; the greater the
> holistic changes attempted, the greater are their unintended and largely
> unexpected repercussions, forcing upon the holistic engineer the
> expedient of piecemeal improvization. In fact, this expedient is more
> characteristic of centralized or collectivistic planning than of the more
> modest and careful piecemeal intervention; ..." (page 69).

Popper also criticises Utopians for their prejudice against accepting the
limits of social control. A priori rejection of such limits violates scientific
method. Worse still, uncertainties concerning human factors force
Utopians to try and control those factors (this being another criticism of

Mannheim, who concerned himself prominently with "The problem of transforming man"; see pages 70 and 89). This removes any possibility of independent tests of the results of Utopian engineering. Such tests must involve assessments as to whether these results suit human needs. If human nature itself becomes the object of planning, then such assessments are impossible. According to Popper, Utopian engineering is necessarily unscientific, therefore.

It is so, on yet another count: its holism. Here, its relationship with historicism (an "unholy alliance") comes in. The argument against holism—its misunderstanding of scientific method—has already been stated in chapter 4. It suggests rejection of holistic planning as well: "Such planning ... is rightly described as 'Utopian', since the scientific basis of its plans is simply nowhere" (page 84). Nor does Popper accept the argument that the holistic method is simply "... the experimental method applied to society" (ibid). Experiments on this scale cannot contribute to our knowledge. The method of all successful engineering, be it physical or social, is small-scale experimentation. This also applies to politics:

"Scientific method in politics means that the great art of convincing ourselves that we have not made any mistakes ... is replaced by the greater art of accepting the responsibility for them, or trying to learn from them, and of applying this knowledge so that we may avoid them in the future." (page 88)

Having dismissed Utopian engineering and centralised planning as unscientific—this quite apart from the monstrous assumption of benevolence on the part of those in control, which, for the sake of argument, he accepts—Popper elaborates further on the advantages of piecemeal social engineering. It can be used to alleviate suffering, which is very different from attempting to realise an ideal blueprint for society:

"Success and failure is more easily appraised, and there is no inherent reason why this method should lead to an accumulation of power, and to the supression of criticism. Also, such a fight against wrongs and concrete dangers is more likely to find the support of a greater majority than a fight for the establishment of a Utopia, ideal as it may seem to planners." (page 91-92)

As will be remembered, this "negative utilitarianism" has attracted the attention of a number of the planning writers discussed in chapter 3. The tendency—with which I agree—is to give it less weight than was given it by Popper.

What Popper adds to these arguments in *The Open Society and its Enemies* is a philosophical justification of rational planning (rooting it in an individualistic, but nevertheless interventionist, theory of the state), the rejection of monist moral theories and the concomitant advocacy of critical dualism, as well as various ideas on the "logic of the situation".

5.2 A Popperian philosophy of planning
A Popperian philosophy of planning can build on his view of man taking
his destiny into his own hands. It is one of his quarrels with both Plato
and Marx that they see it otherwise—though there are important distinctions
between the two on this point. Popper's is an heroic view stressing, as I
do, the responsibility which this implies, as well as the strains which it
creates. Strains notwithstanding, we should not let fate, history, or any
other dark force take it from us.

He not only gives man responsibility for his own destiny, he also
advocates what he describes as rationalism, or the rational attitude, in
discharging it. In so doing, he draws many parallels with science. Because
his preference for rationalism cannot be derived from methodological
argument, it seems only right to subsume it under Popper's philosophy of
planning. In chapter 1, I have already stated what this philosophy
contains, and said that, in Popper's view, it implies a moral choice, much
as my *Planning Theory* does.

Popper's evolutionary theory of knowledge also helps in locating
planning amongst the conscious attempts of man to shape his future.
Chapter 4 introduces this theory, including the parallel which it draws
between organisms developing through natural selection and man discarding
hypotheses through criticisms, describing both as examples of problemsolving. What distinguishes man from organisms is his ability to deal with
symbols, to let hypotheses, rather than living beings, die during error
elimination. In this light, planning may be seen as the search for paths
into the future, discarding those which are undesirable, or even unfeasible.

Popper is often seen as a critic of planning, rather than as one of its
philosophers. But this is only true for the perverted view of planning
which he castigates as Utopian engineering. In this section I have shown
that planning as conscious self-guidance is rooted in Popperian philosophy.

5.3 Popper's theory of the state
Popper's theory of the state relates to this philosophy of planning. It
concerns whether there should be state-intervention, and not planning as
decisionmaking (which is my view). But it also has a bearing on my decision-
centred view, because Popper's trust in politics forms the basis for any
concern for decisionmaking. Only when we assume that, in principle at
least, decisions *can* turn things to the better does it become relevant to
ask for ways in which they are taken. Marx does *not* think so, and
consequently does not concern himself with decisionmaking, yearning
instead for fundamental change. The short account of the current state of
the debate between a 'decision-centred' and a 'control-centred' view of
planning in chapter 2 showed that this argument continues to exert its
influence.

I have noted in chapter 4 that Popper's quarrels with Marx are about theoretical arguments, not about the revulsion felt about unrestrained capitalism. As a consequence, Popper professes himself to be an advocate of just that form of interventionism found in present-day mixed economies:

"... unlimited economic freedom can be just as self-defeating as unlimited physical freedom, and economic power may be nearly as dangerous as physical violence; for those who possess a surplus of food can force those who are starving into a 'freely' accepted servitude, without using violence ...

"... the nature of the remedy is clear. It must be a political remedy ... We must construct social institutions, enforced by the power of the state, for the protection of the economically weak from the economically strong.

"This, of course, means that the principle of non-intervention ... has to be given up; ... the policy of unlimited economic freedom [must] be replaced by the planned, economic intervention of the state ...."
(Popper, 1966, volume 2, pages 124–125)

At this point, Popper sees a fundamental difference from Marx. The latter claims to offer a basis for political action, but that action can only "shorten and lessen the birth-pangs" of the new society. In Popper's view, political power is fundamental. Already in the opening passages of *The Poverty of Historicism* we find this emphasis (stressed in the previous section) on our responsibility for our decisions.

Discussing Marx's concept of the state gives Popper an occasion for expounding his view on the right of people to dismiss their governments. He says Marx underestimates, not only the potentials, but also the dangers of political power, including the power exercised by the proletariat during its dictatorship. But under economic planning of the type preferred by Popper, problems would also occur. He thus formulates a paradox of state planning:

"If we plan too much, if we give too much power to the state, then freedom will be lost, and that will be the end of planning." (page 130)

Popper's theory of the state is individualistic in that it revolves around the rights of individuals and their protection. These rights are not unconditional. There is a "paradox of freedom": where the exercise of the freedom of one individual interferes with the freedom of others, there we have seen Popper thinks control must be exercised.

In this context, Popper distinguishes between two methods of intervention. The one which he prefers is the designing of a legal framework of protective institutions. He claims that this makes the exercise of economic power by the state more transparent and accountable. The other, that is "... empowering organs of state to act within certain limits as they consider necessary for ends laid down by the rulers for the time being" (page 132) is the direct form of intervention Friend and Jessop (1977, page 111) would describe as a *programme*:

"... a set of related future intentions in respect to certain specific situations which are anticipated in the future ..."

Indirect intervention is identical to their notion of a *policy*:

"... a set of future intentions in relation to certain classes of situation; ..." (ibid).

This is, of course, exactly what the law does: specifying what the organs of the state will do if and when a law is broken or an application for subsidy is received.

Popper prefers indirect intervention, much as Hayek does (for a critique of environmental planning in the light of this preference see Hayek, 1960). The reason is that only indirect intervention allows for small adjustments required by the method of trial and error:

"Discretionary decisions of the rulers or civil servants are outside ... rational methods. As a rule ... they cannot even be publicly discussed, both because necessary information is lacking, and because the principles on which the decision is taken are obscure. If they exist at all, they are usually not institutionalized, but part of an internal departmental tradition." (Popper, 1966, page 132)

As against this, a

"... legal framework can be known and understood by the individual citizen ... Its functioning is predictable. It introduces a factor of certainty and security into social life." (ibid)

I am bound to say that the comparative research of Dutch and English planning referred to in chapter 2 leads me to conclude that in the modern welfare state the type of "legal certainty" which Popper advocates cannot be insisted upon. Discretion must be granted lest planning should be condemned to ineffectiveness (Thomas et al, 1983; see also van Gunsteren, 1976). This raises the issue of controlling those in power even more insistently. The outcome of such considerations could be that there should be *less* planning than we have become used to.

5.4 Ends and means in planning

As we have seen in chapter 4, Popper rejects historicist moral theory and advocates critical dualism. This provides a basis for distinguishing between factual and ethical arguments in planning (often expressed in ends–means terms), and between the role of experts on the one hand and politicians and members of the public on the other. But Popper himself does not relate critical dualism to planning. Rather, as with the Popperian philosophy of planning, we must resort to interpreting him.

When discussing Plato's closed society, it will be remembered, Popper draws a distinction between natural and normative laws. The former either hold or do not hold in reality. They cannot be changed at will. But the latter are man-made so that it is possible to change them. This distinction is by no means universally accepted. Many believe that normative laws are also natural in the sense that they are laid down in accordance with, for example, the 'laws of human nature', 'human development', etc. But describing, as Popper does, laws as conventions does not mean

"... that they must be arbitrary, or that one set of normative laws will do just as well as another. By saying that some system of laws can be improved ... I rather imply that we can compare the existing normative laws (or social institutions) with some standard norms which we have decided are worthy of being realized. But even these standards are ... not to be found in nature. Nature consists of facts and of regularities, and is in itself neither moral nor immoral. It is we who impose our standards upon nature ... We are products of nature, but nature has made us together with our power of altering the world, and foreseeing and planning the future, and of making far-reaching decisions for which we are morally responsible." (Popper, 1966, volume 1, page 61)

Decisions can never be derived from the facts, but of course they pertain to facts. Admittedly

"... certain decisions may be eliminated as incapable of being executed, because they contradict certain natural laws (or 'unalterable facts'). But this does not mean, of course, that any decision can be logically derived from such 'unalterable facts'. Rather the situation is this. In view of any fact whatsoever, ... whether it is alterable or unalterable, we can adopt various decisions—such as to alter it; to protect it from those who wish to alter it; not to interfere, etc. But if the fact in question is unalterable ... then any decision to alter it will be simply impracticable; ..." (page 62–63).

Popper then discusses the objection that decisions are themselves facts. This confuses the fact of a decision being taken with the content of that decision. Also, different decisions can be taken with respect to the same fact (this being a further reason why norms cannot be derived from facts).

Though the dualism between natural laws and conventions is essential to our understanding of the social environment, this does not mean to say that all 'social laws' are normative. There are important natural laws of social life also. Popper quotes the laws of economics as an example.

They are connected with the functioning of social institutions and

> "... play a role in our social life corresponding to the role played in
> mechanical engineering by, say, the principle of the lever ... Like
> machines, they need intelligent supervision by someone who understands
> their way of functioning ... Furthermore, their construction needs some
> knowledge of social regularities which impose limitations upon what can
> be achieved by institutions ... But fundamentally, institutions are always
> made by establishing the observance of certain norms, designed with a
> certain aim in mind ... In institutions, normative laws and sociological
> laws are closely interwoven, and it is therefore impossible to understand
> the functioning of institutions without being able to distinguish between
> these two." (pages 67–68)

This equally applies to planning. In the terms commonly used in the
planning literature, we would say that goals cannot be derived from
surveys, but that they are not necessarily arbitrary either. For instance,
they might be tested against other goals.

In particular, it is *not* so that, for the reason that values cannot be
derived from factual statements, Popper would accept any arbitrary value
choice. He is not a proponent of what Habermas (1968) once called
'decisionism', whereby politicians take decisions on questions of value
independently, and experts translate them into concrete proposals
thereafter (see also Popper's reply to Boyle, Popper, 1974b, page 1155).
On the contrary, critical rationalism demands an open form of interaction
between political decisiontakers, their advisers, and those affected.
Allowing for mutual criticism of normative as well as factual assumptions,
as it does, this conforms to the pragmatic model of Habermas.

The possibility of criticising both factual and value propositions is
clearly evident in the quotation below, drawn from the Addendum to *The
Open Society and its Enemies*:

> "... both propositions, which state facts, and proposals, which propose
> policies, including principles or standards of policy, are open to rational
> discussion. Moreover, a decision—one, say, concerning the adoption of
> a principle of conduct—reached after the discussion of a proposal may
> well be tentative, and it may be in many respects very similar to a
> decision to adopt (also tentatively), as the best available hypothesis, a
> proposition which states a fact." (Volume 2, pages 384–385)

When combined with Popper's theory of the state, it is a small step
therefore from critical dualism to participation of the public in decisionmaking. Oppositional practices would gain Popper's approval also, simply
because they increase the chances of criticisms being brought to bear.
This is again interesting, because 'critical theorists' were so very fond of
identifying Popper with 'positivism' during the positivistic dispute, and
of identifying 'positivism' with decisionmaking by technocrats.

These observations will become important when discussing my "politics of rational planning" in chapter 9. Another aspect of critical dualism will concern us before then, in chapter 7. Crucial to it is the view that it is the factual consequences of taking a value position which are of central importance. This is what I shall describe as Popper's consequentialism.

5.5 The logic of the situation

Popper's ideas on the "logic of the situation", being the method of historical interpretation, are perhaps the least obviously relevant for planning. Needham (1977) has already drawn attention to it (calling it by its other Popperian name, the "zero method"; see chapter 3). I think its significance is broader than indicated by him.

Just as with history, we can conceive of planning as the interpretation of situations in which actors find themselves. A difference though is that planning deals with *future* situations.

The definition of the decision situation—being a key-concept of my decision-centred view (see chapter 2)—is then the result of what Popper describes as situational analysis. It refers to unique situations. To describe (let alone to manipulate) situations, one must approach them from the angle of the actor, or actors, concerned. This implies that one can never deal with decision-situations as wholes, as some planners are pretending to do. Synthesis in planning is relative. Planning is more synthetic than analytical disciplines are, but synthesis can never be total, grasping the 'essence' of the situation, or some such.

On all these points I find myself in agreement with Popper. However, my view of planning might run foul of Popper's strictures against methodological collectivism. I have discussed this in chapter 3 and shall return to this topic in chapter 9. Before then (in chapter 7), situational analysis will indeed be shown to be relevant in giving a Popperian account of the definition of the decision situation.

5.6 Conclusions

Popper's views on planning have a decidedly modern ring about them. They go well with the recognition of uncertainties in the planning literature, the quest for alternatives, for flexibility in planning, and for monitoring. Less well known is Popper's support for oppositional practices in planning. Indeed, some of those involved might not wish to be associated with Popperian views, simply because of the 'Popper legend' created by his opponents, that he is a 'positivist'.

Above all, Popper's views underline that blueprint planning has been abandoned for good reasons. Now, in environmental planning, this is associated with an architectural, urban design, or engineering approach, and process planning is accredited to the influence of social scientists. But blueprint planning is not so much characterised by the fact that plans are made by engineers or designers. On the contrary, Popper upholds the approach of engineers, as we have seen. Blueprint planning is rather a question of using a—misconceived—*methodology* which assumes that a complete understanding of the object of planning can—and must—form the basis of firm plans. This is what historicism and holism teach. The object-centred view of planning referred to in chapter 2 is no different. Social scientists holding it perpetrate the sin of blueprint planning, as much as engineers and designers do. Thus, *blueprint planning is not a professional bias of engineers, it is a methodological mistake common to many of those involved in planning (including lay people)*. In Faludi (1982) I show that Geddes, being one of the leading lights in environmental planning, is guilty of it as much as some architects/planners are.

At the end of chapter 3, I said that I was in sympathy with writers trying to find relevance for planning in Popper's methodology of science rather than in his social philosophy. Still, here I give much attention to the latter. But this chapter is still mainly concerned with ideas which Popper himself relates to planning. The next chapter goes beyond this, showing how we can develop planning methodology on *a par* with Popper's methodology of science.

Falsification and the rationality principle

Though clearly inspired by methodological considerations, piecemeal engineering will still be shown to fall short of providing a sufficient basis for planning methodology. So, we must develop a fresh approach inspired by the methodology of the empirical sciences. But I deny that this merely involves applying falsification to planning statements, as some writers discussed in chapter 3 have been shown to argue more or less explicitly. As Popper himself emphasises, it is only applicable to universal statements concerning reality. Whereas planners do *make use* of such statements, or laws, and, naturally, would prefer them to be reliable, establishing their validity is of no concern to planning methodology. The reason is simple: it already forms the object of the methodology of the empirical sciences. The central concern of planning methodology as indicated in chapter 1 is different: to render decisions justifiable. Here, I shall show what this means.

Trying to establish whether decisions are justifiable may sound odd to anybody familiar with Popper, who is squarely opposed to "justificationism". But does Popper not insist himself that methodology belongs to the "context of justification"? Also, does he show enough sympathy for practical decisionmakers who indeed have to justify their proposals? Drawing on Settle (1974), the section after piecemeal engineering will be headed "My teacher's deaf ear". The title of the following one also invokes Settle: "Searching for the 'philosopher's stone'?". It leads to my outline of "A Popperian approach to decisionmaking" in the last section.

6.1 'Piecemeal engineering' is not enough

I agree with piecemeal engineering. The methodological argument on which it rests is negative though. It says how one can *not* plan—in an holistic, or blueprint, fashion. Since all knowledge is uncertain, planning *must* be conducted with full awareness of the possibility of erroneous assumptions invalidating proposals. But, as argued in chapter 5, piecemeal engineering does not necessarily restrict us to small reforms, nor do engineers—whose method of work Popper recommends—restrict themselves to small projects. It is rather a stricture against recklessness in planning, whatever we are concerned with, be it large-scale intervention or detailed plans. The conventional criticism against it, that it is conservative (see amongst others Chadwick's observations reported in chapter 3), I reject. I do so despite my being aware that Popper says that small social experiments help us improve our knowledge. This against the failures of holistic planning, which tend to be so great that they do not teach us anything. But the real issue is not one of the scale at which intervention takes place. Popper's argument is directed against the illusion that we can plan anything "as a whole". We should always proceed experimentally and look out for our mistakes. My problem is that this merely says how we should *not* proceed.

Of course, in encouraging us to look out for our mistakes, piecemeal engineering also has a positive side to it. It improves our knowledge with a view to being better able to intervene in the future. But this is merely a side effect and does not provide us with guidance as to how to proceed in specific instances. Other than that one should "look out for one's mistakes", "eliminate error", "plan within the limits of one's knowledge" and "use experiences gained", piecemeal engineering fails to give any such guidance. It is firm only about the fact that one should not entertain illusions about one's capacity to take correct decisions.

Anyway, what does "error elimination" in planning mean? As Popper himself recognises in the Foreword to Moewes's book discussed in chapter 3, planners cannot experiment like engineers do. Surely, therefore, the analogy drawn between planning and scientific experiments by Dunn (1971) and others (see chapter 3) is loose. The mistakes of planners will emerge only in the future, says Popper in the same Foreword. But a methodology of planning should allow us to assess proposals critically *before* they are put into effect. Then is the time to rectify mistakes without having to suffer adverse consequences.

Once we have absorbed its prudential element, piecemeal engineering loses its meaning. The exhortation to be comprehensive in analysing and evaluating decisions, as long as it is done with due awareness of limitations of knowledge, is equally plausible. Indeed, I can find nothing in Popper's teaching which implies that one should *not* use *all* available knowledge to expand the scope of analysis (this being the meaning which I, for one, attach to comprehensiveness; see chapter 9).

Many think the opposite, namely that the quest for comprehensiveness runs foul of Popper's strictures against holistic, or Utopian, engineering. We have seen in chapter 3 that Gillingwater (1975) and Camhis (1979) have perpetrated the error of identifying rational-comprehensive planning with the positivist assumption that knowledge can be an unambiguous guide to action. But we can be well aware of its limitations and still aim at comprehensiveness.

Of course, I am not saying that piecemeal engineering is of no value to planning methodology. In particular, it incorporates what I shall describe as consequentialism: the principle that, in assessing proposed actions, the expected consequences are crucial. As we shall see, it will take the place of the demarcation criterion comparable with falsification in my scheme of planning methodology.

6.2 Why plans cannot be falsified

Chapter 3 presented the, allegedly Popperian, view that falsification also applies to plans. The clearest statement is to be found in McConnell (1981).

As Dunn (1971) also shows (see chapter 3), plans are statements referring to specific situations: site X ought to be developed in 1995 by building three-storey blocks of flats housing Y number of people, etc. They do not lend themselves to falsification in a Popperian sense.

Now, Popper himself may be partly responsible for this confusion. He talks about "error elimination" as a *general* method of problemsolving (see chapter 5). To planners accustomed to plans going wrong, this strikes a familiar chord, and they then do not draw the distinction between error elimination and falsification. We need to discuss error elimination in planning, therefore, and show that it is not the same as falsification.

When a plan goes wrong, there can be three categories of 'error' committed: the first relating to the—empirical as well as normative—assumptions on which the plan is based, and the second to the logic of the argument leading to the decision to adopt the plan. The third category refers to errors of a different kind altogether: lack of foresight in anticipating that things may go wrong; a failure, that is, to observe the prudence demanded by piecemeal engineering.

Errors in the second or third categories always form reasons for criticism. Errors of the first category are natural for the very reasons which lead Popper to advocate piecemeal engineering. No blame needs to be attached to them. Indeed, I question whether there is even error involved in planning based on assumptions which subsequently prove wrong. Does this invalidate the original plan? Indeed not—it may still be the best plan in view of the situation as originally perceived! (If it was not, then the error committed would fall under category 2 above and we could indeed blame the maker of the plan.) The only thing which has happened is that the perception (in terms of chapter 2: the "definition of the decision-situation") has changed. (Of course, it may be said with reason that the decision-situation should have been defined differently in the first instance, for example that more adequate knowledge has been available, or that more awareness should have been shown of the uncertainty of knowledge!)

Now, it may still be relevant to learn from mistakes *without* apportioning blame. But there is the further point that learning takes the form of error elimination only where *empirical* assumptions are concerned. Goals can *not* be assessed in this way. They are always specific to whomever holds them. All we can learn from their not being held any more is that the decisionmaker has changed his or her mind—or perhaps that somebody else calls the tune now, so that other goals prevail. This is not the same as eliminating an error.

It is not even so that learning from such errors as have been made always has beneficial effects on future decisionmaking. Maybe the policy has changed altogether so that better knowledge is of no relevance any more. Or maybe a decision—whether right or wrong—has so changed the situation that it is irrelevant to assess the assumptions on which it was based, simply because no such decision will ever be taken again. The Eastern Schelde flood barrier in the south of The Netherlands is only built once. The knowledge, with hindsight, that the same level of safety could have been achieved at less cost by improving existing dikes is irrelevant once the point of no return has been reached.

Beware of facile arguments about the importance of learning from plans going wrong, therefore. Such learning requires careful analysis of the categories of 'error' committed. Only some errors lead to anything comparable with error elimination in the empirical sciences. It is under restricted circumstances only that the implementation of a plan can be compared with an experiment, and where this happens, this is a sideshow. Never can experimenting be the main purpose of a plan. That purpose is to do whatever is correct in a given situation.

Even if we did finally regard the implementation of a plan as an experiment, that plan could never be falsified in Popper's sense. What may be falsified is a hypothesis on which it is based. Plans are not theoretical statements, they refer to *unique situations.* In terms of chapter 4, they take the place of basic statements, and not of hypotheses.

Plans cannot be falsified, then, but they can still—and must—be *justified.* The next section will demonstrate that, as far as planning is concerned, the quest for justification need not be the heresy which it may sound to Popperian ears.

6.3 My teacher's deaf ear

Here I am departing from my policy of not referring to the secondary literature on Popper. My excuse is that Settle (1974) is uniquely relevant to my concern. He discusses induction and probability and their relation to a "rational guide of life":

> "... many philosophers of science see the vulgar demand for a guide of life as a demand for a vindication of rational decisions. To this cry for bread, Popper has turned a deaf ear. To my teacher's deaf ear, I turn a blind eye—and join in the new quest for a philosopher's stone: I want a solution which is consistent with—and even suggested by—Sir Karl's solution ..." (Settle, 1974, page 704).

Settle claims that Popper has neglected many aspects of the application of his ideas and wishes "... to try to characterize (even if only crudely) the rationality implicit in science so as to aid the construction of a guide of life based on science". Similarly, I search for a way to justify decisions which is consistent with Popperian critical rationalism.

After extolling the achievements of science and technology, Settle states:

> "The popular view is that induction is the method of science and that the solution to the problem of induction will provide the prize in the quest for a guide of life based on science." (page 700)

He claims that Popper's rejection of induction is too austere and that Popper "ignores technology". Settle's own definition of technology is identical to my concept of rationality: the selection of the right 'hypotheses' to act upon. Only, I would not have referred to hypotheses but rather to alternative courses of action. Anyway, choosing the right 'hypotheses' is not the same as induction:

> "Inductivists usually present the problem of induction as the problem of choice between rival hypotheses as bases for action and subsume the appraisal of the truth value of an hypothesis as a special case of that choice; they know that positive evidence is relevant to rational decisions how to act—every judge, every banker, every insurance agent knows that much—and they conclude that it must be relevant to judgements of truth of general hypotheses." (page 703)

Settle's central point is that probability (of desirable consequences, that is) and induction (of truth from observations) can be unfused (hence the title of his paper: "Induction and probability unfused"). Their relation does not concern me here. What does is that, in interpreting probability, Settle refers to *standards of responsibility*. He gives examples where a decision procedure looks rational in one case and not in another, depending on the character of the particular *case*:

> "Rational decision making consists not only in using standard procedures but, crucially, in picking out which procedure is appropriate. The central problem in the search for a guide of life is to find an overarching procedure which teaches us, amongst other things, how to pick out formal procedures as appropriate to particular cases ...

> "Happily, there is such a procedure and it is already in use ...

> "... it is standard practice for scientists to engage in critical debate ...

> "It seems to me that a basic requirement of rationality is that no position, procedure, theory, person, institution or document be regarded as sacrosanct ... Further it is a fact of life that no argument could be convincing unless the premises of the argument were accepted, or agreed upon, as true, and the logical structure of the argument, as valid. For rational discussion we need agreements which are themselves held to be corrigible. If 'partial justification' means arguing from agreed premises by an agreed procedure, and if 'partial reliability' were defined as a characteristic of the conclusion of such arguments, then I can see nothing intrinsically anticritical in partial justification and partial reliability—on the contrary, I think they are indispensable as components in a rational guide of life ..." (pages 711-712).

Settle goes on "... to show that the requirement to be *responsible* according to certain agreed upon but corrigible standards follows rather naturally from the application of the *critical attitude* to specific practical goals". He is really talking about planning:

"If one's aim is growth of knowledge, then imagination is called for in conjecturing, and toughness is called for in testing; but if one's aim is designing an aeroplane ..., quite apart from the ingenuity called for in research and design, a great deal of imagination and persistence will be needed to think up and try out all possible ways in which the plane could fail to function ... The desire not to endanger the lives of future passengers ... is a sufficient reason for taking precautions; ..." (page 714).

In the first instance, boldness is the order of the day—and justification in the sense of trying nothing else but proving that one is right to be abhorred. In the second instance, trying to prove that one is right in putting a proposal forward is all the game is about.

Settle also refers to the analogy between rationality and the standards of responsibility in politics and life generally. He shows that the urge to take precautions is a public requirement. He then asks:

"But ... is the existence of standards of responsibility consistent with the theory of rationality as critical debate? At first sight, it might appear not. If the standards of responsibility are equivalent to permissions to cease from critical debate, then there may be an incompatibility between the use to which the standards are put and the critical attitude. On the other hand, standards of responsibility may themselves be subject to critical debate ... If the attitude to the standards is critical, it is not anticritical to have standards." (pages 714–715)

Settle relates this view of rationality to Popper's original demarcation problem. Popper's solution, falsificationism, is in need of modification. As we have seen in chapter 4, it is an answer formulated in 1919–20 to the problem of distinguishing between Einsteinian physics and Freud's and Marx's theories. Later Popper extended it to science generally. But Settle claims there is "... much in science remarkably different from what Popper understood Einstein to be doing".

Instead of the demarcation between science and nonscience, Settle would rather distinguish between rational and irrational disciplines, treating science as a special case of a rational discipline:

"In a general way, science could, I suppose, be characterized by the long term goal of systematically explaining experience and by a standard of responsibility which requires the empirical testing of scientific theories. Technology, which sometimes appears to be rendered almost non-scientific (and hence not really respectable) on Popper's characterization of science, is then given status as a rational discipline, which has standards of responsibility as empirical and as tough as 'pure' research but is distinguished from 'pure' by its prime goal. Francis Bacon already made this distinction in *Novum Organum*: To understand nature and to conquer her." (page 721)

Schilpp's volumes, where Settle's paper is published, include Popper's reply. He is complimentary but points out that he *has* dealt with practical problemsolving. His answer comes down to identifying the "most characteristic task of technology", or problemsolving, as being "to *point out what cannot be achieved*", giving examples of the technological form of empirical laws first referred to in *The Poverty of Historicism* (see chapter 5). This is a useful reminder of his teaching, but it falls short of a methodological rule concerning practical decisionmaking—which is what Settle (and I) are looking for. I think Popper recognises that Settle's comments are fair. Popper sees critical rationalism, not only as an approach to the problems of science, but as an attitude to life. Settle merely searches for the implication of this view: the 'philosopher's stone' or guide to practical decisionmaking.

6.4 Searching for the 'philosopher's stone'

In searching for Settle's 'philosopher's stone', we should have an idea as to what it should look like. Naturally, it must be applicable to *decisions*. Therefore, it must be adapted to their nature. In chapter 2, I defined decisions as statements committing actors to certain actions.

The rule must also allow *criticism, both* of the factual *and* of the value assumptions on which decisions rest. It must, furthermore, invite criticism by *others*, based on Popper's maxim: "I may be wrong and you may be right ..." (see chapters 1 and 4). It must do so by making clear the grounds for decisions.

Above all, the rule must allow decisionmaking to become a rational discipline in Settle's terms. Again following Settle's ideas, this must lead to the formulation of standards of responsibility as tough as those imposed in empirical research.

It is necessary also to make clear what we can *not* expect such a rule to do. We should *not* ask of it that it should *remove limitations of human knowledge.* This is the reason why, although we must be clear about where our arguments are *not* based on analysis, that fact alone forms no cause for rejecting any decision. As we have seen in chapter 4, the assumption that no assumption at all needs to be made is evidence of what Popper calls uncritical rationalism. The making of assumptions is simply necessary in all forms of argument, including that concerning decisions.

Nor can we expect our rule to *do away with conflicts of interest,* or with *people being stubborn.* We must not expect this rule to be *always observed in practice* either. Dogmatism continues to exist, but this is no proof for it being inescapable.

These being the outlines of the rule for which we are looking, I now turn to formulating it in a way which is strictly analogous to Popper's approach to the empirical sciences.

6.5 A Popperian approach to decisionmaking

In describing my Popperian approach to decisionmaking, I start from a situation of people engaging in dialogue concerning a decision. We assume that they aim to defend it by argument. This assumption is inherent in this being a methodological discourse. Methodology concerns the justification of propositions, including proposals for decisions. It belongs to the "context of justification", as Popper has it (see chapter 1).

Certainly, a critic might question the very assumption that decisions should be justified. But he who denies the need for justifying decisions and sees intuition and sheer commitment as sufficient grounds for taking them, places himself outside the context of methodological discourse.

If this sounds like ruling other views out of court, then so be it. I cannot conceive of methodology based on intuition and commitment. This is not a squabble over words. If somebody wishes to define methodology in such a way that it does include intuition, he can have his way. I am then simply not interested in his methodology but in the one which does depart from the need to adduce arguments.

I certainly do not want to claim that there is *no* role for intuition in decisionmaking. There is, but this does not make intuition—and even less commitment—into a sufficient base for *taking* decisions. My rejecting this is based on the authoritarian and anti-intellectual connotations pointed out by Popper (see chapter 1) of any position which puts emotion above dialogue.

Obviously, this is a value judgement. It coincides with Popper's preference for argument and his rejection of irrationalism. I do not accept it without reasons. The consequences of irrationalism sketched out by Popper in *The Open Society and its Enemies* (see chapter 1) are disdainful. Only if we were disproved in this our view, that is, if irrationality would demonstrably lead in practice to less violence than rationalism, then Popper and I would have to think again. Until then, we stick to our preference.

It will be remembered from chapter 4, that Popper arrives from his preference for rationalism at falsificationism by virtue of the following argument: if you are seeking truth, you can do no better than falsify your hypotheses. If you have a number of them, each falsifiable, then the one which has passed the most stringent tests and/or runs the greatest risk to be falsified in future is the one you should choose.

This indicates how a Popperian rule for decisionmaking should be formulated, namely by indicating the regulative idea in decisionmaking (equivalent to that of seeking truth in the empirical sciences) and by formulating a demarcation criterion for distinguishing acceptable from unacceptable proposals (just like falsifiability), together with a criterion for choosing between such acceptable proposals as can be formulated (like the rule that one should prefer theories which have been subjected to the severest tests). Both demarcation criterion and decision rule must clearly reflect the aim of decisionmaking, viz: the regulative idea, analogous to the idea of seeking absolute truth in the empirical sciences. All this in the spirit of *rationalism* with its preference for argument.

Before attempting to justify a decision according to this rule, the situation to which it refers must be described. In chapter 2, I introduced the term "definition of a decision-situation" for this. Definitions of decision-situations show great variation. But the demarcation criterion and the decision rule, much as the regulative idea, all apply irrespective of the definition of the decision-situation. At this point, of course, the distinction between substantive and procedural theory of planning (see chapter 1) re-emerges. The question of how to justify a definition of the decision-situation is different from that of which rule to apply to the justification of decisions. A definition of a decision-situation is a description of whatever one chooses to view as problematic and should be transformed into a new and better state by means of deliberate intervention. Thus, a definition of a decision-situation can be justified by defending the choice of beginning and end points of the intended process of change, and by demonstrating that the action proposed will indeed have the desired effects. The choice of beginning and end points is a normative issue. The claim that an action will have a desired effect ultimately rests on empirical knowledge.

In defining decision-situations, one must pay due regard to the context in which that decision is made, who makes it, which means are at his/her disposal, etc. Students discussing their choice of study may refer to the value of certain degrees and their capacities for following various courses. They base themselves on examples of relatives and friends who have graduated in the past. Perhaps they avail themselves of advice by careers tutors. They bring all this to bear on their decision with the aim of finding the best course of study for them.

There is an analogy here with Popper's description of the judicial process (see chapter 4). He distinguishes between the *verdict* of the jury being "an answer to a question of fact" and the sentence of the judge. The first is a decision to accept a certain description as being true. (It is a description, though, which depends on the legal situation. Thus, it is not "objective"!) This decision forms the basis for applying the system of the criminal law.

The definition of the decision-situation can be compared to the verdict of the jury. To accept statements as representing a truthful description of the decision-situation means taking a decision in turn. It is taken with a view to applying the decision rule. Having such a definition is a precondition even of applying it. In this way, the decision rule and the definition of the decision-situation are closely related.

There is also an analogy with testing hypotheses. This is to be expected. Popper discusses verdicts as being analogous to experiments. A description of an experiment is informed by the falsification rule, and such a description is a precondition of applying that same rule, just as I said the definition of the decision-situation was a precondition for applying the decision rule. Also, without experiments, falsification would be meaningless as a rule. But experiments and falsification are still conceptually different, just as I distinguish between the decision rule and the definition of the decision-situation.

With the definition of the decision-situation out of the way, we can turn to the final assault on the Popperian decision rule. Popper has no ready-made answers. He refers frequently to the ethical aspects of decisions, in particular in *The Open Society and its Enemies*. The acceptance or rejection of moral criteria, or standards, certainly involves decisions. Practical decisions in planning rest on many such standards, but more is involved. Think of a road proposal where, in addition to (moral as well as technical) standards, empirical knowledge is brought to bear. Also, the form of a road proposal is different from a statement proposing a standard. A practical proposal is not a matter of pronouncing on what is to be considered as morally good or bad, but of relating general principles and knowledge to a specific situation, resulting in a statement of what ought to be *done*, there and then.

Nevertheless, Popper's discussion of standards provides the entry point for bringing this exploration to its conclusion. He compares standards with empirical propositions. As with propositions, there is a regulative idea about proposals to adopt standards. It "... can be described in many ways ... , for example by the term 'right' or 'good' " (Popper, 1966, volume 2, pages 384 – 385; see also chapter 7 below). The same goes for the practical decisions with which I am concerned. We should simply aim at good, right, or correct decisions, no less than that! "Correct decisions" is the regulative idea on which the methodology of planning should orient itself—knowing, of course, that this aim is as distant as that of attaining truth.

But what demarcation criterion and what decision rule does this imply? Here I anticipate arguments developed more fully in chapter 7.

One of the occasions of Popper discussing decisions is described in chapter 1 when talking about his reasons for accepting 'rationalism'. Ultimately, as we know, Popper sees this as a matter of taking a moral decision, but he also describes what the consequences would be of opting for the alternative, namely irrationalism. Popper would certainly agree that not only moral, but practical decisions as well, should be taken with *a view to their consequences*. Actually, this is implied in 'piecemeal engineering' which argues that one should pay regard to the—expected as well as unexpected—consequences of our actions.

Based on the above, the demarcation criterion which I propose is this: to make sure that we work towards correct decisions (the 'regulative idea'), we must always pay regard to the *consequences* of proposed actions. Arguments in support of decisions which fail to state their consequences must be ruled out of court as being inconducive to the aim of correct decisions. Thus, 'consequentialism'—the insistence that we should only accept proposals, the consequences of which are stated as fully and explicitly as possible—fulfils the same role as does the falsification rule for empirical propositions: it separates statements about decisions which do lend themselves to being rationally assessed from others. (The term 'consequentialism' is culled from Regan, 1980, who thinks it a better one for what is commonly described as utilitarianism; see also chapter 11.)

It is useless protesting that it is difficult to know the consequences of actions. The same holds true for the falsification of hypotheses. In chapter 4, this has been described as forming the subject of frequent disputes between scientists: the problem of 'basic statements'. As with falsification, ultimately, consequentialism also comes down merely to the requirement of consistency: you cannot continue to argue for a decision, once you have recognised that it will have unacceptable consequences, much as you cannot hold on to a general law whilst at the same time believing that a basic statement contradicting it is also true.

In any one situation, there may be many decisions which have been analysed in terms of their consequences and thus fall within the demarcation criterion. To discriminate between them, we need a criterion of choice: the decision rule. It is that practical decisions should be taken by *comparing* the consequences of their alternatives. To be more precise, *all* consequences of *all* alternatives need to be considered and the best one chosen. In this way, the chances of a decision being criticised, and possibly rejected, are maximised: every time a realistic alternative to a proposed decision is advanced and/or a consequence is pointed out, neither of which have been considered by the decisionmaker, that decision needs to be reconsidered. This is in keeping with the spirit of critical rationalism.

Now, this decision rule is exactly what the planning literature describes as rationality. In chapter 2, it figures in the decision-centred view of planning. It has been shown to rest on the demarcation criterion of consequentialism, which does for decisions what falsification does for empirical hypotheses. The decision rule fulfils the role of Popper's criterion for choosing between different hypotheses which are falsifiable, but as yet not falsified. In presenting it in this way, I do not claim to give a new formulation to rationality. I merely seek to clarify its nature as the decision rule compatible with—and indeed suggested by—Popperian teaching.

6.6 Conclusions
The core question of this book posed in chapter 1 has been answered. It asks for the central methodological rule to apply in decisionmaking and planning, a rule which fulfils the same function in planning methodology as does falsification in the methodology of the empirical sciences. In this light, many discussions concerning rationality might be deemed resolved.

It is *not* a prescription for how to *make* plans. It is a methodological rule and relevant only to their acceptance or rejection; in other words, to their justification. (But in telling planners what this involves, it does of course influence how they make plans, that is, it informs planning methods.) Also, rationality—being a criterion for choosing between decisions—rests on another rule which is not made explicit in the planning literature: the demarcation criterion of consequentialism. Whether explicit reference is made to the expected consequences of proposed actions separates decisions which can be defended from those which cannot.

Discussions on rationality mostly do not concern its nature as a methodological rule, but whether it is 'idealistic' at present to aim for rational decisionmaking. In chapter 11, I shall show that this is a recurrent comment on Popper's philosophy as well. But methodology cannot answer such questions. Only when you choose to argue about decisions (as I believe one should), then rationality applies. Whether one can actually *do* so, or whether, owing to the prevailing power structure, the outcome is a foregone conclusion, is a different question. In answering it, one must assess the chances of rational discussion in the particular situation at hand.

Popperian building blocks for the definition of decision-situations

In this chapter I shall show that Popper's ethics are indeed consequentialist, and how he would define decision-situations.

Popper's consequentialism can be deduced from his reasoning in favour of 'rationalism' discussed before, from his critical dualism, his views on technology, and his "law of unintended consequences". As regards defining decision-situations, we must attend to his view on how historians interpret events by performing situational analyses. (As to the adequacy of such an interpretation, Popper himself introduces a rationality principle in the form of the assumption that actors act in their own best interest as they see it. This is supportive evidence for the critical-rationalist character of my decision rule presented in chapter 6.) Also, there is an analogy between the definition of decision-situations and the interpretation of experiments: just as the interpretation of experiments (rather than the underlying hypothesis) can be rejected, if we do not like the outcome, we may decide to change the definition of the decision-situation.

In discussing that definition, I shall also take account of Popper's theory of problemsolving. The analogy with the 'problem-centred' view of planning discussed in chapter 2 is superficial. My decision-centred view is more compatible with Popper's theory of problemsolving.

7.1 A consequentialist ethics
In previous chapters I have explained Popper's view that falsification helps approaching truth asymptotically, and that a rule should be found which stands in a similar relationship to the regulative idea of correctness of proposals for decisions. I have also said that indications in Popper's work as to the nature of such a rule are few and far between. One is where he invokes, as we have seen, the *consequences* of irrationalism as reasons for accepting 'rationalism' (see chapters 1 and 6). I have said that I assume that practical decisions, in Popper's view, should be taken in a similar manner. This is what consequentialism involves. In chapter 11, I shall show that it represents one of the schools of thought in ethics, hence the title of this section: "a consequentialist ethics".

The case for characterising Popper's ethics as consequentialist is strengthened when we attend to his critical dualism, the doctrine of the use of empirical laws in their technological form and the "law of unintended consequences". This is what this section is about.

Critical dualism—already discussed in chapter 5—rests on the impossibility of deriving values from facts. This has been demonstrated in Popper's critique of monistic theories of value (see chapter 4).

Now, Popper does *not* mean that any value position is acceptable. Rather, he is concerned that we should not subscribe to relativism, describing it in the Addenda to *The Open Society and its Enemies* as the main philosophical malady of our time. A definite relationship exists between facts and values.

"... our decisions [to adopt standards] must be compatible with the natural laws (including those of human physiology and psychology) if they are ever to be carried into effect; for if they run counter to such laws, then they simply cannot be carried out ..." (Popper, 1966, volume 1, page 62).

As we have seen, when adopting rationalism, Popper forges that link via the consequences of adopting value positions, and this is what I concentrate on here. Apart from cases where the consequences of adopting some value position are such as to make them unfeasible, there are others where different value positions have conflicting consequences, making it necessary to choose between them. These, then, are the various implications of critical dualism.
where Popper compares proposals and propositions and the role of regulative ideas. Earlier I showed that there is a very similar regulative idea underlying practical decisionmaking: to do the right thing. Here, the learning aspect of trying to do so occupies the centre of the stage. Much as with absolute truth, of which we can never say whether we have achieved it, so with proposals. We shall never be able to decide definitely as to whether we have formed an absolutely valid proposal for a decision. But we can make progress, much as Popper says we can approach truth, as well as good standards, in asymptotic fashion:

"As in the realm of facts, we can make discoveries ... These discoveries create standards, we might say, out of nothing: as in the field of factual discoveries, we have to lift ourselves by our own bootstraps. This is the incredible fact: that we can learn; by our mistakes, and by criticism; and that we can learn in the realm of standards just as well as in the realm of facts." (1966, 1st published 1945, volume 2, page 386).

Clearly, such learning goes via finding out about the consequences of decisions. This is done either before or after decisions are taken. In the first instance, we seek to identify their *expected* consequences. This is ex-ante evaluation. In the second, we try to measure real consequences after the fact. This is ex-post evaluation. In both, the consequences of decision are what it is all about. Critical dualism drives on identifying and analysing them. This is why Popper's adoption of critical dualism supports my characterising his whole outlook on decisionmaking as consequentialist.

In learning, not only about the world around us, but also about our values (including, as we have seen, the invention of new ones to meet new situations), Popper's ideas on empirical laws being applied in their technological form, discussed in chapters 4 and 6, play their part. This relates to the logical argument leading to his falsificationist principle:

"The theories of the natural sciences, and especially what we call natural laws, have the logical form of strictly universal statements; thus they may be expressed in the form of negations of strictly existential statements or, as we may say, in the form of non-existence statements ...

"In this formulation we see that natural laws might be compared to 'proscriptions' or 'prohibitions'. They do not assert that something exists or is the case; they deny it. And it is precisely because they do this that they are falsifiable. If we accept as true one singular statement which, as it were, infringes the prohibition by asserting the existence of a thing ... ruled out by the law, then the law is refuted ..." (Popper, 1959, page 68–69).

In *The Poverty of Historicism*, Popper expands this into considerations of technology. Its most characteristic task is to "*point out what cannot be achieved*" (Popper, 1961, page 61; see also chapter 5):

"This way of formulating natural laws is one which makes their technological significance obvious and it may therefore be called the 'technological form' of a natural law." (ibid)

The importance of any empirical law in its technological form is that it can be expressed "... by sentences of the form: 'you cannot achieve such and such results' or perhaps, 'you cannot achieve such and such ends without such and such concomitant effects'." (ibid)

In other words, empirical laws—to the extent that they are deemed reliable—*exclude* the taking of certain decisions, but they can never indicate which decisions must be taken. In a manner of speaking, knowledge indicates the area of freedom within which decisiontakers can pick and choose according to preference. In my terms: it circumscribes the definition of the decision-situation. It does so by way of predicting the consequences of proposed actions, just as the doctrine of the application of laws in their technological form demands. What is underlying is, of course, consequentialism: the ethical theory that decisions must be judged by their consequences. Empirical laws in their technological form merely provide instruments for doing so.

This is what happens in zoning land-use: where an area subject to flooding is hatched on a map as being unsuitable for building purposes, this is a shorthand way of saying: "You cannot build on land which is subject to flooding", or "You cannot build on land subject to flooding without accepting that your building will be damaged at regular intervals". The same applies to the application of man-made laws relating, for example, to the preservation of areas of outstanding natural beauty. The hatching of such areas on land-use maps is again but a shorthand way of saying: "You must not build in areas of outstanding natural beauty, otherwise their amenity will be threatened (and, if you do, then the authorities will serve an enforcement notice demanding that the building should be removed!)"

The last element of Popperian methodology reflecting his consequentialism is what Popper calls the "law of unintended consequences". It is not an empirical law but a guideline. Actions have unintended consequences. Our knowledge is limited and we cannot fully understand whatever we act upon. So, we can never be sure of the real consequences of our actions. Therefore, Popper urges us to look out for unintended, as well as intended, consequences (which is what ex-post evaluation of plans referred to above is designed to do). Now, if decisions to adopt plans were not to be judged by their consequences, then there would be no point in looking for unintended ones. In this way, consequentialism underlies the law of unintended consequences.

This law of unintended consequences is already present in Popper's notion of a social technology (Popper, 1961, pages 68-73). It is stated in more extended form in *Conjectures and Refutations*:

"... it is one of the striking things about social life that nothing ever comes off exactly as intended ..." (Popper, 1963, page 124).

From this, Popper draws conclusions regarding the task of social theory, viz

"... to explaining how the unintended consequences of our intentions and actions arise, and what kind of consequences arise if people do this that or the other in a certain social situation." (op. cit., page 125)

Popper's consequentialism is one of the reasons why the rationality rule seems in accord with his philosophy. But in chapter 6 we have seen that rationality goes beyond consequentialism. The latter is merely a demarcation criterion, whereas rationality is a criterion for choosing between alternative proposals. The law of unintended consequences supports the opinion that this is Popperian also. It is contained in the rationality principle insisting that *all* consequences—intended as well as unintended ones—need to be considered.

But maybe rationality conflicts with Popper's theory of problemsolving. Maybe his theory of problemsolving is more in accord with 'muddling through', or 'disjointed incrementalism' (see for example, Camhis, 1979, quoted in chapter 3). It is necessary, therefore, to hold rationality against the light of Popper's theory of problemsolving.

7.2 Popper's theory of problemsolving
For many years, planning has been seen as problemsolving also. Popper himself talks in terms of problemsolving (see chapter 5). Yet, in chapter 2, I said that my current decision-centred view departed from the object-centred or problem-centred one. Clearly, I have some explaining to do.

What is Popper's theory of problemsolving? In chapter 5, I touched on his views of living beings as engaged in continuous problemsolving (his evolutionary theory of knowledge). He is concerned not only with practical problems (such as planning theorists are when talking about problemsolving) but also with theoretical problems. This leads to his claim that theories must be regarded as —tentative—solutions to problems.

But Popper would never suggest—as the object-centred or problem-centred view of planning does—that one could *start with* an objective analysis of 'the problem', and search for optimal solutions afterwards. Such a procedure would run foul of his teaching that even facts are theory-laden. Problems cannot be defined 'objectively' either. Rather, any problem definition reflects the perspective of the planmaker (and, hopefully, that of his clients), including what he—or they—can *do* about problems. In other words, in planning, a 'problem definition' in the spirit of Popper's teaching is really a *definition of the decision-situation*, as outlined in chapter 2 (see also my discussion of Needham, 1982, in chapter 3).

The decision-centred view can easily be squared with Popper's that every theory can be seen as a rational solution to a problem. In planning we should read for 'theory' 'plan', and for 'problem' 'decision problem'. Put this way, I subscribe to planning as problemsolving. But in view of prevailing misconceptions concerning planning as problemsolving, which make it look similar to the object-centred view of planning, and so as to avoid any misunderstanding, I decided to abandon this term.

It would be unfortunate if my decision-centred view of planning should conflict in some other way with Popper's theory of problemsolving presented in chapter 5. But this is also not the case.

In his essay, "On the theory of the objective mind", Popper (1973, pages 153–190) concerns himself with interpretations of human actions by means of his scheme of problemsolving progressing from a tentative theory via error elimination to a reformulation of the original problem (see chapter 4). The idea of a comparative evaluation of alternatives is clearly present, as is the notion of problemsolving as a cyclical process. (Indeed, the description there reads much like one of the applications of strategic choice of the Institute for Operational Research; see chapter 2.) What is absent is my demand that, for an interpretation of, in my case, a decision-situation to be satisfactory, *all* alternative 'conjectures' must be considered.

Instead of imposing such stringent requirements, Popper describes a satisfactory interpretation as one that "... can throw new light on new problems ... we may say that we can gauge the progress we have made by comparing P1 with some of our later problems (Pn, say)" (page 165). Admitting that problems regularly shift and change, in planning much as in other forms of problemsolving, I find it unsatisfactory, nevertheless, to identify success in planning merely with shifting problems. But we must take into account that Popper is mainly interested in knowledge and its growth.

So, it is understandable that he lays such great store by *new* problems: they open up new perspectives. But in practical problemsolving (or decisionmaking), clearly, we sometimes wish to know that *existing* problems can be solved, to the best of our knowledge anyway.

Popper might have dealt with this issue, too, and not only with the growth of knowledge. (In chapter 6, I have shown Settle to be similarly concerned about Popper's lack of interest in practical problemsolving.) In so doing, he might have invoked his own doctrine of searching for unintended consequences (see above). Better still, he could have asked for *all* consequences—intended and unintended ones—to be evaluated. Also, he should have made the conditions under which solutions to problems would be accepted more stringent than he actually has, by adopting my demand that *all* alternative 'conjectures' (all alternative courses of action) should be assessed in this way. If he had taken these steps—as I believe he would if only directing his attention to the matter—then his rule for regarding a problem as solved would be identical to my rationality rule for decisions.

There seems to be no conflict, then, between Popper's theory of problemsolving and my decision-centred view, the less so since I can give a Popperian account of one of the central concepts of this view: the definition of the decision-situation.

7.3 A Popperian account of the definition of the decision-situation
The reason for referring to Popper's concept of the "logic of the situation" (sometimes also called "situational analysis" or the "zero-method"; see my comment on Needham in chapter 3 and also chapters 5 and 6) in the context of an argument about planning methodology is threefold. First, situational analysis is the analysis of *unique* situations. As argued previously, in planning, too, we deal with unique situations. Second, in connection with situational analysis and its derivatives, Popper himself invokes a rationality principle—being the central rule of planning methodology. Third, there is a parallel—already hinted at in chapter 6—between my definition of the decision-situation and Popper's views on the interpretation of experiments (this being a specific instance of analysing unique situations).

In *The Poverty of Historicism*, Popper shows how a historian explains historic events:

"... undoubtedly there can be no history without a point of view; likewise the natural sciences, history must be selective unless it is to be choked by a flood of poor and unrelated material ...

"The way out of this difficulty is, I believe, consciously to introduce a preconceived selective point of view into one's history; ... this does not mean that we may twist the facts until they fit into a framework of preconceived ideas, nor that we may neglect the fact that does not ...

But it means that we need not worry about all those facts and aspects which have no bearing upon our point of view and which therefore do not interest us." (Popper, 1961, page 150)

Elsewhere, Popper describes this as situational analysis starting from an explicitly chosen point of view depending on the situation concerned. In his Autobiography, he gives the following account:

"By a situational analysis I mean a certain kind of tentative explanation of human action which appeals to the situation in which the agent finds himself ... we can try ... to give an idealized reconstruction of the problem situation in which the agent found himself, and to that extent make the action 'understandable' ... that is to say adequate to his situation as he saw it." (Popper, 1974a, page 179)

As of history I have said of planning, in chapter 5, that it involves interpretations of the situations in which actors find themselves. For planning, as for the study of history, it is also true that, without a selective point of view, one obtains *too much* information. This is *the* shortcoming of the doctrine of 'Survey – Analysis – Plan'. The choice of a point of view must be made *in advance* of conducting research, instead of the other way round (which is where I find myself in complete agreement with Taylor, 1980; see chapter 3).

There is also a difference, of course. Planning deals with *future* situations which are thus imaginary. Better still, since historians also imagine situations (sometimes, the term retrodiction is used to denote that this is so), we should say: planning deals with situations which are the objects of *volition*. No matter how much imagination is involved in historical research, we cannot sensibly will the past to have been different from what it has actually been. In contrast, to will the future to be different from what it might be without intervention is the whole point of planning.

This distinction will become important in due course. Here we pause to conclude that Popper's situational analysis also applies to planning, that is to say he would judge a plan by the same standard as the interpretation of actions in the past: by its adequacy to the situation of the actor. In the terms of the decision-centred view: he would judge a plan by its adequacy to the definition of the decision-situation.

As to Popper's invoking a rationality principle in connection with situational analysis, this already occurs in *The Open Society and its Enemies*. The method of historical interpretation

"... besides the initial conditions describing personal interests, aims, and other situational factors, such as the information available to the person concerned, ... tacitly assumes, as a kind of first approximation, the trivial general law that sane persons as a rule act more or less rationally." (1966, volume 2, page 265)

Apart from summing up the various elements of which an historical interpretation may consist, elements which we would also find in any definition of decision-situations, there is thus talk of a general principle which allows one to make sense of the way these elements are related to one another to provide a coherent account—which is exactly how I see rationality. Popper's invoking the rationality principle is further evidence, therefore, for the Popperian character of the interpretation offered in chapter 6.

Popper's fullest statement on rationality in connection with situational analysis is to be found in his later work. Koertge (1979) provides a reconstruction of the explanatory scheme involved, comparing it with schemes of Hempel and Dray and expressing concern about the status of Popper's rationality principle as a "trivial empirical law". This we need not share because of the difference, as indicated above, between historical explanation and planning. In historical explanation, it might indeed be necessary to assume that something like a rationality principle prevails as a matter of empirical fact, otherwise an explanation in terms of the logic of the situation becomes unthinkable. It is then perhaps fair to ask, as Koertge does, that this assumption should be subjected to tests, as other empirical propositions are. But in the case of planning, rationality does not refer to how men *do* behave, it is a postulate about how they *ought* to take decisions. As Popper never grows tired of explaining—and as Koertge no doubt would accept—'is' and 'ought' statements are logically independent from each other.

So, Koertge's worries about the empirical status of Popper's rationality principle need not affect its use as a methodological rule in planning. But there is, anyhow, reason to doubt Koertge's interpretation of Popper's use of the rationality principle. Since this throws light on the way in which Popper sees the application of the concept of the logic of the situation, I relate his discussion of Collingwood's method of "subjective re-enactment" in his essay "On the theory of the objective mind". There he quotes Collingwood describing how a historian attempts to understand the situation of a subject—using the Byzantine emperor Theodosius as his example—by re-enacting his *experience* in his own mind. Popper thinks that re-enacting is not the right word:

> "The historian's analysis of the situation is his historical conjecture which in this case is a metatheory about the emperor's reasoning. Being on a level different from the emperor's reasoning, it does not re-enact it, but tries to produce an idealized and reasoned reconstruction of it, omitting inessential elements and perhaps augmenting it. Thus, the historian's central metaproblem is: what were the decisive elements in the emperor's problem situation? To the extent to which the historian succeeds in solving this metaproblem, he *understands* the historical situation.

"Thus what he has to do *qua* historian is not to re-enact past experiences but to marshall objective argument for and against his conjectural situational analysis." (Popper, 1973, page 188)

Based on this, Koertge might have come to the conclusion that situational analysis was a mere construct in the analyst's mind. Popper's reference to the rationality principle as a "trivial empirical law" might then have to be dismissed as a somewhat loose formulation. This principle is simply the basis on which to perform situational analysis. As such, it need not be empirically true.

Be this as it may, as far as planning is concerned, situational analysis necessarily involves reconstruction of the decision-situation. The aim is to enable those concerned to decide for themselves as to whether they can agree with any proposal at hand. That this reconstruction is done *rationally* is but a—necessary—assumption. If the assumption was *not* made, then the attempt to analyse a plan, and to criticise it on that basis, would be useless. Criticisms could always be countered by saying that the plan was not meant to be a rational response. Clearly, this would make planning into a pointless exercise.

The last element of Popperian methodology which is relevant to the definition of the decision-situation is his view about how experiments are interpreted.

As described in chapter 4, in many situations it is by no means easy to decide whether an experiment leads to the rejection of a hypothesis. Thus, falsification is problematic. But Popper says that scientists, on the whole, are able to agree on the issues involved. They are able to judge the appropriateness of any auxiliary hypotheses involved, as well as of the entire experimental set-up. In any case, as we have seen, all that falsification says is that one should be consistent. Thus, one cannot hold a hypothesis to be true and at the same time accept that something exists which, according to the same hypothesis, must not exist. So, the interpretation of experiments, instead of the hypotheses, may be wrong.

The parallel with defining decision-situations is as follows: whenever we are dissatisfied with the results of planning, it may be that the definition of the decision-situation is up for change. That definition is itself the result of numerous choices, in much the same way as the interpretation of an experiment is. Clearly, any one of them might be questioned, but these are considerations of a different order than the acceptance or rejection of the decision flowing from the definition of the decision-situation by way of applying the rationality rule. It is important that one keeps this distinction in mind. Most arguments in planning concern the definition of the decision-situation. The worries which many express about rationality are perhaps misdirected. Rationality is a straightforward rule. As such, it need not be controversial. Controversy should rage over how to define decision-situations.

7.4 Conclusions

I have come to the end of my exposition of the main proposition of this book, namely that rationality is the centrepiece of a Popperian planning methodology. My arguments rest on his views about the role of methodology and the function of rules therein, stated in chapter 1. In a paper published not so long ago (Faludi, 1983), I even claimed that rationality was the exact equivalent of falsification, that is a demarcation criterion. As we have seen, I am now differentiating between the demarcation criterion of consequentialism and the decision rule of rationality.

In this chapter in particular, I have demonstrated also that my view of planning as decisionmaking does not conflict with Popper's theory of problemsolving, and that what he says about situational logic, and the role of the rationality principle therein, supports this proposition. In the final analysis, a definition of the decision-situation is analogous to the interpretation of scientific experiments in that it, too, is a—fallible—reconstruction of a specific situation resting on many assumptions and decisions. We are under no obligation to accept this reconstruction. But if we do, then the requirement of consistency demands that we draw our conclusions accordingly. In the case of an experiment, the conclusions relate to whether we accept the hypothesis to which the experiment relates. In the case of a definition of a decision-situation with respect to a plan, it relates to acceptance of the plan which flows from it.

Decisionmaking, planning, and "World 3"

In the previous chapter I took a Popperian approach to defining the decision-situation. In this chapter I continue this line of thought, building on Popper's later philosophy, in particular on his concept of a "World 3" of objective knowledge and his views of the role of language.

Whether we are concerned with a single decision, or with sets of interrelated decisions (the latter being the case in planning), the decision-centred view puts great emphasis on the definition of the situation which is the object of concern. Popper's notion of a "World 3" of objective knowledge—as against World 1 (material objects) and World 2 (subjective experience; see chapter 4)—helps in interpreting the definition of the decision-situation as a construct of the mind. Once expressed, it acquires an existence of its own and can be criticised by others.

Popper's views as to the interaction between his three worlds can be shown to be of relevance to planning methodology, in particular to the issue of *flexibility*. As part of this argument, I shall also touch upon difficulties of communication in planning, an aspect to which Popper does not give attention.

8.1 Planning without a planning subject?

Often, planning seems a far cry from any subject charting its course in deliberate fashion. Of course, it is easy to allocate formal responsiblity. But who is the real planning subject? The Council adopting a budget, the Minister issuing guidelines? We know that, behind these terms, complex processes hide and that the results are often a far cry from a coherent plan of action.

Looking at planning in the real world, it seems decidedly attractive, therefore, to shed the idea of planning by a planning subject. When talking about networks and reticulists, Friend et al (1974) seem to be driven by similar thoughts. Lindblom's (1965) mutual adjustment—which they adopt all too uncritically (see Faludi and Mastop, 1982)—seems a prime example of 'planning' without a planning subject.

Now, in view of Popper's theory of *knowledge without a knowing subject*, one might perhaps conceive of planning without a planning subject. At first glance, the existence of a knowing subject is an assumption for any theory of knowledge as self-evident as that of a planning subject for planning methodology. Yet, as we know, in his essay on "Epistemology without a knowing subject", Popper (1973) has done away with it (see chapter 4). Let us then see whether we can do the same with the planning subject! Practising planners—and planning theorists alike—would then be relieved of having to answer any such questions as: 'Who is responsible?' 'Whose goals must form the basis of planning?' 'Which consequences need to be taken into consideration?' 'What is the legitimacy of planning proposals?'

All these pressing issues are related with our present topic: 'How can we identify the planning subject?' Take that concept away, and the problems disappear at a stroke. Planning simply becomes a free-for-all where everything goes.

8.2 The definition of the decision-situation as a World 3 construct

I shall discard this line of thought, but taking the reader through the argument is the best way of exploring the implications of Popper's theory of knowledge. The latter holds, the reader will remember, that the products of our minds, as soon as we have parted with them, acquire an existence of their own. In this sense, they then become objective. These objective products of our minds inhabit Popper's World 3.

Amongst them are decisions. Indeed, Popper explicitly describes decisions as World-3 objects, for instance:

"... the decision whether or not to accept an invitation to lecture, in addition to much work in hand. The acceptance letter, and the entry into the engagement calender, are World 3 objects, anchoring our action programme; and the general principles we may have developed for accepting or rejecting such invitations are also programmes, also belonging to World 3, though perhaps on a higher hierarchical level." (Popper and Eccles, 1977, page 126)

Definitions of decision-situations are World-3 objects also. They must be communicated to others, otherwise no argument can develop about the decision in question. A definition of a decision-situation—being a relatively complex statement—is also made up of other, more elementary, World-3 objects: descriptions of possible courses of action and of their expected consequences, expressed in diagrams, texts, mathematical symbols, etc. I shall turn to the language aspect below. In defining a decision-situation, these World-3 objects must be ordered in such a way that we understand the decision under consideration.

Now, to differentiate between such a definition of a decision-situation and Popper's all-embracing World 3, one might describe the former as a situation-specific segment of World 3. Majone (1980, page 158) refers to it as the "policy space": "a subset of Popper's World 3".

Popper (1973, pages 153 – 190) does something similar. He relates his recent theory of knowledge to his earlier concept of situational analysis, writing about a "problem situation" as focusing relevant segments of World 3 on the explanation of specific situations. This extends to include the *application* of knowledge as well. It will be obvious to the reader that my "definition of the decision-situation" concept does the same.

But World 3 knows no knowing subject. In expressing our ideas in a form accessible to others, we turn them into common property. Ideas, problems, theories belong to all of us. Also, everybody's thought products are admitted to World 3. Is the same true for situation-specific segments of World 3? Then we could indeed eliminate the planning subject from planning methodology. It would be as superfluous as the knowing subject for Popper's theory of knowledge.

8.3 The necessary assumption of a planning subject

Every situation has an infinite number of aspects. The consequence is that an infinite number of statements can be made even about the simplest situation. This is also true for decision-situations—only more so, because they are far from simple. They involve—inherently uncertain—predictions and affect many—often conflicting—interests! So, the offer of building blocks for the definition of any decision-situation is infinite. But nobody has the capacity to deal with more than a limited amount of information at once. So, it is impossible ever to complete the job of defining even the simplest decision-situation. But do not forget that such a definition remains a precondition of making a well-considered choice.

Of course, what it all comes down to is that decisionmakers must be *selective* as regards those aspects of decision-situations to which they attend. Therefore, the distinction between what is, and what is not, *relevant* is what distinguishes its situation-specific segment—which I call a definition of a decision-situation—within Popper's all-embracing World 3. In that world there is no need for selectivity other than by discarding elements that have outlived their usefulness. (Even these remain in World 3, forming a sediment on which the living World-3 objects prosper.) For the rest, all utterances about the real world form legitimate World-3 objects.

One can also tackle this issue in another way. Theoretically, the number of angles from which any given situation could be approached is infinite, or, in other words, there is an infinite number of 'relevances'. There is, then, also an infinite number of ways of defining the same decision-situation, and all are legitimate World-3 objects. This is exactly why a choice must be based on the relevance of competing definitions.

But relevance cannot be decided upon *in general.* Something is always relevant to *somebody*, and not to others. *This somebody is the planning subject.* Just because planning is concerned with what to do in *specific* situations, *the existence of a planning subject forms a necessary assumption in planning.*

This does not change the fact that planning practice shows little resemblance to decisionmaking by agents acting deliberately on the basis of a well-understood plan. Planning often reminds us more of an uncontrolled stream of events with many participants pursuing their own ends. This is why Meyerson and Banfield say the planning process in Chicago

"... resembled somewhat the parlour game in which each player adds a word to a sentence which is passed around in a circle of players: the player acts as if the words that are handed to him express some intention ... and he does his part to sustain the illusion." (Quoted by Banfield, 1959, included in Faludi, 1973, pages 143–144)

Of course, the planning subject need not be a real person. It can be imagined; but it cannot be missed. Every time two or more decision areas are related to each other (which is where planning stems from; see chapter 2), we think about them *as if* they concerned one and the same subject. (By the same token, to look at several decisions as if they concerned one and the same subject has *no other* meaning than to attend to their interrelations.) For example, awareness of global ecological inter-dependencies has led to the notion of a 'spaceship earth', of the need for some form of concerted action, at peril of destroying the ecological balance on our planet; awareness of limited resources has led to concern for future generations and to notions of sustainable development, etc.

The assumption of a planning subject is particularly helpful when seeking to find out what is involved in understanding a plan. I shall first state Popper's view on how we grasp World-3 objects generally. Contact with their material manifestations is far less important than the mental process of reconstructing these objects:

"According to my view, we may understand the grasping of a World 3-object as an active process. We have to explain it as the making, the re-creation, of that object. In order to understand a difficult Latin sentence, we have to construe it: to see how it is made, and to re-make it. In order to understand a problem, we have to try at least some of the more obvious solutions, and to discover that they fail; then we discover that there is a difficulty—a problem. In order to understand a theory, we have first to understand the problem which the theory was designed to solve ...

"... In all these cases the understanding becomes 'intuitive' when we have acquired the feeling that we can do the work of reconstruction at will, at any time." (Popper and Eccles, 1977, page 44)

How can one reconstruct a definition of a decision-situation—being the World-3 object I am here concerned with? Only by assuming that there is a planning subject, and by looking at the situation through *his* or *her* presumed eyes!

This also goes to show what it means to give others insights into a decision-situation—the most important precondition of democratic decisionmaking. They must be given the opportunity to reconstruct that decision-situation for themselves. At the same time, democratic procedures demand of the participants the honest attempt to do the reconstruction job from the point of view of the assumed planning subject.

This does not mean that they have to *accept* that point of view. Nothing at all is said about which point of view should prevail, about who and what the planning subject should be. Where there is conflict in planning, this often revolves around this very issue: in whose name and for whose sake do we plan? But none of this concerns me here. The purpose of this argument has only been to show that it is necessary to have a planning subject as a theoretical construct, when we think about, talk about, and strive for any kind of planning.

Where does this leave planning practice in all its disorderliness? Do coalitions not split up frequently? How often does it not happen that a plan evaporates when it comes to implementation? But from a methodological point of view, so what? The unstructured stream of events simply has the upper hand. To be sure, individual actors may still plan for their own ends. They define *their* decision-situations against the backcloth of their appreciation of what that stream holds in store for them.

Why, then, does this image of an unplanned stream of events worry us at all? First because we wrongly think that methodological assumptions—like that of the existence of a planning subject—must somehow meet the test of reality. When we then find that no such thing as a planning subject exists in fact, we are inclined to blame this on that concept. But another conclusion is equally plausible: that there is very little planning, simply *because* there are no planning subjects endowed with the cognitive capacity and political muscle to plan. So, the concept of a planning subject becomes a yardstick against which to measure practice.

Second, assuming even that some actors show some capacity to plan, it is only with difficulty that we can conceive of *societal action* as such as being planned. However, this is what we often understand planning to be. Seen in this light, it is a condition of planning that somebody—the state, the government, the leader, the party, etc—should have an overview, should guide and plan. It is this assumption which makes us think that there is something wrong when we cannot discover any overarching planning, or the concomitant planning subject for that matter.

But we need not share this view. I, for one, talk about a planning subject only where planning in the sense of some coordinated attack on a number of interrelated decisions is actually being attempted. This is rarely the case with societal action on a large scale. Maybe that such action should never be attempted. After all, whatever action we take in the name of whichever subject, we should take it with full awareness of its consequences—and of the consequences of its alternatives. In short: we should decide on our actions rationally. If this demonstrably cannot be done, it is perhaps better to abstain from acting altogether.

So, it is consistent with a Popperian point of view to retain the planning subject in the sense that every effort at planning implies a definition of the decision-situation, and every such definition a subject whose point of view prevails. This definition may be seen as a situation-specific segment of World 3. To the extent that planning as an activity requires the construction of such a world, we may also say: planning is the manipulation of World-3 objects, or symbols, for the purpose of formulating new World-3 objects (rules, programmes, statements of intent, maps), each having a purpose deriving from the planning subject—be it real or imagined. Ultimately, these rules, programmes, etc must have an effect on the material world (World 1), via the actions which they inform.

8.4 Difficulties of communication

It is clear that language is fundamental to planning. In chapter 4, I showed the importance attached by Popper to language in his evolutionary theory of knowledge. In this section, I attend to the difficulties of using language in defining decision-situations—in constructing a situation-specific World 3, as it were.

It may seem beside the point to consider difficulties of communication in a work concerned with methodology. However, where there are recurring problems in living up to methodological rules, there they become legitimate objects of methodological concern. Many examples of this can be found in Popper's writing. For instance, his strictures against holism may be seen as a reflection of limitations of our knowledge: we can never understand anything 'as a whole', so we must not even attempt to do so!

In this spirit, I shall look at communication in general, and concept formation in particular. Concepts denote aspects of reality. At the same time, there is an enormous gulf between the concepts which we use and reality. This is impossible to overcome. Concepts will never be identical with reality. There are always various ways to conceptualise it. The difficulties of communicating across disciplinary boundaries, between experts and lay people, and between people with different social and political backgrounds, bear evidence to this.

The conventional answer is that we must carefully define our concepts. But when we do, the problem hits us even more forcibly. This is because definitions themselves are valid only within a particular context. Every definition uses other terms to explain the one being defined. Obviously, they themselves can be defined in turn. But somewhere the process must come to a halt. This is where so-called undefined terms come in.

Whether people do share a definition depends on their sharing these undefined terms—on whether they attach the same meanings to them. Yet, words can mean different things to different people. The meanings which we attach to terms depends on our experiences, on how we have dealt with what they denote in the past. So, there is a difficulty. Popper's World 3 is far from coherent.

Ackoff and Emery (1972) and Archibald (1980) deal with these problems. The former define communication as a way in which one system affects "... the other's parameters of choice without changing either its environment or the components of its choice situation" (page 142) by providing (a) information resulting in changes in probabilities of choice; (b) instruction resulting in changes in the efficiency of choice; or (c) motivation resulting in changes in relative values. We could also say: communication is that by which an actor affects the other's definition of his/her decision-situation.

Difficulties of communication become apparent where Ackoff and Emery discuss signs as the main conveyors of communication. A sign is "... anything that is a potential producer of a response to something other than itself" (page 161). It carries signification, that is "... something other than the sign that the sign potentially produces a response to" (ibid). Popper would say: signification is the World-3 aspect of a sign.

Ackoff and Emery then distinguish between denotation and connotation. Denotation refers to "... the set of objects or events signified by a sign" (page 164), connotation to "... the set of properties (of the objects or events responded to) that produces the response" (ibid). Together, these are sometimes referred to as the meaning of a sign. Thus, 'fire' means different things, depending on the situation, and 'matches' has different connotations, depending on what qualities of matches one is thinking about—reasons for why I said above that words may have different meanings to different people. Ackoff and Emery concur:

"... a sign may have different meanings for different individuals, or different meanings for the same individual at different times ... 'No rain is expected today' may mean one thing to a farmer at work but another when he is vacationing." (pages 170–171)

This throws light on the problems that we started from: how to arrive at a definition of the decision-situation between a number of individuals. They have to do with the different denotations and connotations of signs to different individuals—or to the same individual in different situations.

Archibald (1980) discusses pitfalls of analysis in problemsolving which result from the inadequacy of words, confirming what has been said above: "... the meaning of a word depends on more than the immediate context in which it appears" (page 179). Words "... are often plurivocal ..." (ibid). The 'interpretative disciplines' have been trying to tackle this problem for a long time. In proposing that policy analysis—in our terms: planning—should be viewed as an interpretative science, Archibald quotes Unger:

"... interpretative disciplines must also deal with the ambiguity of meaning peculiar to the phenomenon of consciousness. Every act of speech ... has a meaning ... given to it by ... the original speaker ... Yet this meaning must always be rediscovered by an interpreter, who has his own purposes and his own form of existence ... The resolution of the ambiguity of meaning is possible to the extent that interpreter and interpreted participate in the same community ... of shared beliefs ..." (page 189).

We may conclude that, for a plan to be effective in guiding action, there is a *necessary* and a *sufficient* condition, both having to do with communication. The first is that there should be a *community of discourse* embracing all those concerned. The second is that there should be *agreement* as to the definition of the decision-situation.

A community of discourse may be achieved by exchanging formal communications and/or by face-to-face interaction. The latter is the path advocated by Friedmann (1973) with his "transactive planning", its European counterpart being "communicative planning" (see van Gunsteren, 1976). Formal communication is effective only where there is little need for mutual understanding, simply because it already exists.

But where a community of discourse is absent, it needs to be established. Such a community can only be established by—discourse! A meeting between commanders and subalterns is a discourse much as a planning appeals procedure is. In the end, the meaning of exchanges and of their consequences should be more easily understood by all those concerned. They should begin to share a common World-3 construct concerning the situation they are faced with.

Beyond this, the effectiveness of plans as frameworks for action (this being the view of effectiveness that befits my decision-centred view of planning) depends on whether the planmaker can either compel those concerned to adhere to the plan (turning them into mere instruments of his will), or arrive at an understanding with them, so that they regard the plan as their own. Then they cannot but follow it, thus making it truly effective. This is why agreement as to the definition of the decision-situation has been described as a sufficient condition of effectiveness in planning (but one which will hardly ever be fully achieved).

Where does this leave World 3, the world of objective knowledge? It is a world which exists *independently* of us, and is—or should be— accessible to all. Now, if definitions of decision-situations—being concepts— can be understood only by an in-group of those who have participated in their formulation, then they seem neither independent of us, nor accessible to all. Thus, there is a problem.

The phenomenon of an in-group, with its own shared meaning attached to concepts, is common in planning. Every working group experiences difficulty in conveying its understanding to others. In a different context, Popper recognises this, namely where it comes to the interpretation of experiments. He leaves the ultimate judgement as to the validity of basic statements to the scientific specialists concerned.

This all enforces the point made in the previous section about *relevance* as a criterion for determining the definition of the decision-situation and about the assumption of a planning subject in deciding on issues of relevance. (It also underlines the difficulties of planning.) Understanding a plan is reserved for those who, in a sense, are *part of it*: who form part of the planning subject. This includes those who reject plans with reasons. They, too, must first have assimilated the language in which it is expressed, so that they form part of the community of discourse around it. Following a plan voluntarily presupposes not only this community of discourse but also agreement as to the definition of the decision-situation.

8.5 Plastic control and flexibility

The comments above give rise to the following: in looking at how a plan functions as a framework for action (see chapter 2), one must recognise that (a) this involves communication, and (b) unless the planmaker and the actor concerned are one and the same (this being rarely the case), the issue arises of how the intentions of a plan are conveyed to the latter. Some intentions of plans will always be misunderstood. Actors will always feel that the plan does not relate to *their* situations, as *they* see them. Worse still, as Archibald shows, there will always be ambiguity surrounding the very meaning of the plan. Meaning must be rediscovered every time a plan takes effect in influencing action. At that point, actors will bring to bear their own perspectives. The eternal struggle between planning and implementation bears evidence to this. It makes it inevitable that plans should undergo change during implementation. This is why implementation is a poor term anyway, suggesting mechanical fulfillment of the purposes of a plan. I much prefer to talk in terms of operational decisionmaking (see chapter 2).

The problem can also be expressed as the problem of flexibility. We need to be keenly aware of the fact that, however hard we try, plans can at best exercise a form of 'plastic control' (see Gillingwater and Hart, discussed in chapter 4). The best they can achieve is some influence on the thinking of the actors concerned. Certainly, one cannot expect plans to *determine* their actions in any detailed way.

Another way of stating the problem is this: one of the axioms of the decision-centred approach is that planmaking is distinguished from decisionmaking in that the former deals with clusters of interrelated decisions in their totality. This immediately distances planmaking from operational decisionmaking, both in terms of time (planmaking must occur *before* operational decisions are being contemplated), as well as in terms of their locations in their organisational context. The problem of flexibility, then, is to bridge the gap between them. That gap results from uncertainty during planmaking about the real situations in which the ensuing decisions will be taken. Bridging the gap can be done by postponing and/or delegating as much as possible. Therefore, plans should be loose frameworks to be filled in later, as and when the need for specifying them arises. This is best done by the actors concerned. After all, it is *their* choices which planning must help to improve! In so doing—and this is what 'plastic control' means—they reinterpret the plan in the light of the concrete situation at hand. Nobody should be under any illusion that 'better planning' or 'more teeth' for statutory planning authorities can change this.

8.6 Conclusion

The fact that planning often seems a far cry from a planning subject charting its course in deliberate fashion formed my starting point. Can planning methodology perhaps do without it, much as Popper has eliminated the knowing subject—a "subjectivist blunder"—from the theory of knowledge?

I approached this question by looking again at the definition of the decision-situation. It forms part of Popper's World 3, the world of objective knowledge. It is that segment of World 3 which is relevant to the decision at hand. Specifying it presupposes that one knows in whose name planning is done: the planning subject. If planning practice shows little evidence of this, then it simply means that there is little planning going on. It does not invalidate the claim that a planning subject is a necessary assumption in thinking about planning.

Planning in the name of some planning subject involves dialogue. How can it be fruitful? Words mean different things to different people. Nevertheless, a community of discourse is a necessary condition for the effectiveness of planning—the sufficient condition being agreement concerning the definition of the decision-situation.

There is always a problem in conveying the meaning of a plan, in particular to the actors involved in 'implementation': the 'consumers' of plans. This conclusion has focused attention on flexibility in planning. A plan must be adaptable to the situations at hand. Control exercised by a plan over operational decisionmaking should therefore be 'plastic'.

This is where the exploration of the relevance of Popperian philosophy to planning methodology comes to an end. Before summarising the results and discussing possible criticisms in Part 3, I shall look again at the final part of *Planning Theory*.

"The politics of rational planning" revisited

The reader will remember that criticisms of *Planning Theory* coming from professed critical rationalists—in particular Eric Reade—renewed my interest in Popper. In chapter 1, I argued that the overall concerns and approaches of that work can be reformulated in remarkably Popperian fashion. In this chapter I specify this claim with respect to proposals therein concerning "The politics of rational planning", where I indicate principles which planners should follow so as to be able to plan more rationally.

There follows a summary of my previous argument. After that, I shall tackle the most obvious criticism which could be levelled against it by a Popperian: my advocacy, at that time, of rational-comprehensive planning. Rational-comprehensive planning may be thought to be subject to Popper's strictures against Utopian, or holistic, engineering. After some skirmishes in previous chapters, I shall deal a blow to this myth, spread even by such perceptive reviewers of the literature as Leach (1982). Comprehensiveness is worth pursuing for a Popperian.

Next, my idea of simultaneously fostering comprehensiveness and criticism will be compared with the teaching of Popper, as will four principles put forward therein for the organisation and procedures of planning. The final section is a discussion of Reade's critique of my initial position. It will be interesting to see whether his challenges to the type of normative theory which I advance are founded in Popper's philosophy.

9.1 "The politics of rational planning"

The central aim of my previous work was to formulate testable hypotheses. Except for saying that this alone should recommend it as Popperian, it need not concern us here.

The hypotheses I proposed contain a number of contextual variables: the scope and range of controls exercised by a planning agency, the role accorded to planners, etc. I then raised the question of whether planners should merely adapt their style of planning to the prevailing planning environment, or whether they should attempt to make the latter more conducive to the planning style which they prefer. I point out that, as a group, planners can, and very often *do*, have a *policy* towards planning and the planning environment. Hence "The politics of rational planning".

Its aim is that planning should be rational in the sense of evaluating comprehensively all alternatives; that these considerations should include alternative goals; that planning should respond flexibly to new situations. But none of this can actually be achieved, not for one hundred percent anyway. Still, we can approximate this ideal by division of labour in what I call 'multiplanning agencies'. Even here, one must be sceptical because of problems of coordination. It is an illusion that these can be dealt with merely by devising sophisticated information systems.

It is intriguing to find out how multiplanning agencies work. Their overall direction, or strategic planning, should attract particular attention. It is obvious that this planning must refrain from becoming involved in detail, leaving that to others more intimately concerned with the substantive problems at hand. Now, this begs the question as to what the strategic elements are, a question which can be answered only from case to case. Besides, I argue in *Planning Theory* that strategic planning should also keep an eye on the performance of the entire multiplanning agency. In this way, strategic planning introduces an element of self-awareness in planning, which should increase rationality.

Developing multiplanning agencies and strategic planning is the first principle of the politics of rational planning.

The next two relate to the organisation of planning. The exploration of real alternatives requires committed planners. They must not see themselves merely as the loyal servants of their political masters, as the bureaucratic model stipulates. (In fact, where that model is followed, bureaucrats often pursue their own policies and attempt to manipulate politicians accordingly.)

Demanding that planners should be allowed, and indeed encouraged, to engage in political argument does *not* mean that their role becomes identical to that of politicians. In *Planning Theory* I draw on Friend and Jessop (1977) differentiating between decisionmaking and decisiontaking. They argue that decisionmaking should involve open discussion between all those concerned, including professional planners of course. Decisiontaking involves the shouldering of political responsibility. Clearly, the expectation is that, in assuming their responsibilities, officials will be able to benefit from the full and open discussion which Friend and Jessop envisage during decisionmaking. To engender it by rescinding the bureaucratic concept of the planner's role is the second principle of the politics of rational planning.

The third merely expands upon it. Discussions should not be limited to exchanges between the bureaucratic top and politicians but should extend to all echelons. Party factions should be encouraged to join forces with groups of planners, thus making sure that *alternatives* can be analysed for their feasibility and consequences. In this way, we might prevent planning agencies with all their expertise developing policies which bear the stamp of their chief planning officers.

From here it is but a small and evident step to laying planning open to being influenced by those affected. Looked at in this way, participation, too, is a means of further increasing the range of options considered, and of the scope of criticism in planning. This is the fourth and last principle.

The aim is that, by participating in planning, those affected come to feel more subjects than objects of planning. Ideally, control should take the form of persuasion. This must be preferred over the use of regulatory powers and material incentives. Persuasion should be combined with an approach by which one merely sets a *framework* within which other actors can choose freely.

These ideas build on those of Etzioni (1968). The reader will no doubt think that they have a naive ring about them. Persuasion assumes some form of consensus. As pointed out in the previous chapter, planning is often characterised by conflicts of interest. Participation, more often than not, results in greater awareness of these.

But participation is not less desirable for all that. To formulate plans which those affected perceive as their own remains an ideal, and participation the means for achieving it. We merely conclude that participation tends to raise the issue of whether the preconditions for democratic decisionmaking exist. But any exploration of whether our democracies are able to resolve conflicts which, thanks to participation, become more apparent, would take us far beyond the scope of my work.

We should not be surprised. That attempts to increase the rationality of planning ultimately pose the radical question of whether ours is a rational society is to be expected. I have accepted no a priori limits to the scope of rationality. The concept of 'human growth', being the rationale of planning theory (see chapter 1) raises the same issue. Clearly, though, we cannot expect to *answer* them on the basis of planning methodological argument alone. Our assessment of present society, and of the limits to rationality which it imposes, plays an important part.

As we shall see in chapter 11, this touches upon a persistent criticism levelled against Popper's social philosophy: its alleged idealism.

9.2 Is it Popperian?
The idea behind the "politics of rational planning" is to foster criticism whilst simultaneously maintaining the drive towards comprehensiveness in planning. Superficial understanding of Popper might easily lead one to conclude that this idea runs foul of his strictures against 'holistic' engineering. This is not the case. The four principles of the politics of rational planning, as set out in the previous section, do not conflict with critical rationalism either.

Popper's strictures against 'holistic', and his advocacy of 'piecemeal', engineering are based on the conclusive argument that the former cannot be achieved (see chapter 5). But in chapter 6, I already indicated that this is all that there is to piecemeal engineering. Beyond warning against recklessness, it does not provide any positive guidance. I also said that a prudent application of the seemingly un-Popperian exhortation to be comprehensive in the generation and evaluation of alternatives is in fact compatible with his teaching. This conclusion rested on the observation that it is all too easy to comply with piecemeal engineering. After all, *no* analysis can be holistic; therefore *all* analysis is piecemeal. Popper himself points this out where he draws attention to the phenomenon of 'unplanned planning' in centralised systems (see chapter 5). But clearly, we want to *surpass* existing practice. The quest for comprehensiveness raises our sights and keeps the essential tension in planning.

There, I also explored the implications of *not* insisting on planning being comprehensive in its analysis: the basis for *criticising* planning proposals would *disappear*. As long as action is considered in the light of *some* of its consequences, the answer to *all* criticism could be: "Sorry, folks, but I have been piecemeal!" It is only because we attempt to be comprehensive—and expect others to do the same—that such criticisms become meaningful. Thus, comprehensiveness in analysing alternatives and their consequences—which is the meaning attached to rational-comprehensive planning, at least since Banfield introduced urban planners to the relevant arguments (in Meyerson and Banfield, 1955)—is necessary from a Popperian point of view.

There can be no objection to pursuing other aims of the "politics of rational planning" either, such as consideration of alternative goals, and flexibility in adapting to new circumstances. Nor can the 'four principles' be faulted as un-Popperian.

The formation of multiplanning agencies so as to enable coordinated attacks on problems (the minimum one may ask for is that decisions of various agencies should not be at cross purposes with one another!) is the most direct expression of the quest for comprehensiveness, yet I can see nothing un-Popperian in it. Of course, I am aware of the widespread disappointment concerning all-out efforts at coordination using, for example, Planning–Programming–Budgeting Systems, and that the necessary negotiations between the many agencies and interests concerned turn out to be time consuming and frustrating. For the sake of effectiveness, one is right to question the usefulness of such 'comprehensive' approaches. But we know that comprehensiveness needs to be tempered by prudence, that due account must be taken of limitations. Strategic planning is largely concerned with how to balance such limitations against the desire for comprehensiveness.

Lest I should be accused of negating the substantive aspects of planning, I hasten to add that this involves analysis both of the issues which one considers as in need of attention, as well as of the strengths and weaknesses of the institutions of planning, leading to self-consciousness. Again, I can see nothing wrong, from a Popperian point of view, with advocating self-conscious attempts to reach beyond the constraints of the present situation, for as long as they are based on a mercilessly honest appreciation of one's limitations in so doing.

The second principle of free exchanges between planners and politicians, together with the third extending this to all echelons of planning organisations, allowing for coalitions between planners and outside political interests, are both designed to encourage the practice of critical dualism which Popper advocates (see chapters 4 and 7), exempting neither factual information nor value positions from criticism. Also, the prerogative of politicians to take decisions underlines the Popperian doctrine that decisions never derive from judgements of fact alone.

The distinction between decisionmaking and decisiontaking runs parallel with the Popperian one between the context of discovery and the context of justification. Decisiontaking belongs to the context of justification. Next to the soundness of arguments, what is at stake here is the legitimacy of committing a public agency to certain lines of action. But where proposals *come* from, how they have been formulated, by whom and with which ulterior motives, is of no relevance for whether one should accept them. As we have seen, for Popper this is a reason for not being interested in discussions of what he calls "psychologism": considerations of the thought processes involved in science. For me this is a reason for saying that there is no justification in barring anybody at all from participating in decisionmaking. The chances of successful criticism can only improve by planning proposals being looked at from various points of view *before* they lead to firm commitments.

The importance attached by Popper to the preconditions of criticism can be gleaned from Part 4 of *The Poverty of Historicism*. There, he describes his "institutional theory of progress". Objectivity, he argues, rests upon the public character of science "... which imposes a mental discipline upon the individual scientist ..." (Popper, 1961, page 155). The preconditions of criticism need to be maintained, and this also applies to politics and planning:

"Holistic control, which must lead to the equalization not of human rights but of human minds, would mean the end of progress." (page 159)

The fourth principle of the politics of rational planning, preferring persuasion and framework planning as ways of exercising control, is not only an argument for flexible and democratic planning—which in itself should recommend it as Popperian—it is also the least repressive of criticism. The reservations in the previous section concerning participation should not deter us from drawing this conclusion. Where conflict prevails, Popper would be the last to be surprised by the fact that such a desirable form of planning cannot be implemented. Based on his theory of intervention (see chapter 5), he would reluctantly agree to the use of minimal political power, instead of mere persuasion, so as to prevent individuals from interfering with each other's freedom.

At this point it is useful to reiterate that there is also a difference between Popper's views and mine. The reference above to his reasons for accepting intervention clearly expresses his methodological individualism. In chapter 3, I relay that I find it unconvincing as a *methodological* principle. What is deemed an unacceptable interference with our freedom as individuals is *socially* determined, and it varies from situation to situation.

Both Americans and Britons—whose Atlantic civilisation Popper so ardently admires—accepted stringent controls on their freedom during World War II. Churchill proudly relates that no other warring nation, whether his allies or the axis-powers, achieved the same degree of mobilisation of the population for the war-effort as Britain. Clearly, the balance between individualism and collectivism was different then from what it is today. Nor would it be easy to argue for such exertions on the basis of individual preferences. There were nations at war defending different principles. Now, if the limits to individual freedom, and to admissible interference with it, are socially and situationally determined, what point is there in clinging to methodological individualism?

9.3 The critique by Eric Reade

Most of Eric Reade's points revolve around my normative planning theory. He has also singled out for criticism my use of Mannheim's notion of substantive rationality. I accept as valid his points concerning my use of this concept, but reject his criticism of normative planning theory.

Reade's position is epitomised by his parable of two books found in the ruins of the building of The Royal Town Planning Institute after the Great Obliteration in 1990: *Keeping Theory* and *A Reader in Keeping Theory* (Reade, 1976). Research by puzzled archaeologists had shown, so the tale goes, that park keepers concerned about their professional status had debated the theory of park keeping as an activity. Later they had turned to seriously considering the quality of grass instead, so that their parks could withstand trampling so much better. Clearly, this refers to procedural versus substantive theory (see chapter 1).

Thus, Reade denies that the step from knowledge (such as about grass seeds) to action (say about sowing them in specific quantities and areas) involves problems of its own. This amounts to a rejection of the usefulness of looking at decisionmaking in planning and the methodological issues which it raises.

Reade objects to normative theory of planning in particular. He takes exception to my work, saying that "... those who provide such normative theories, due to their understandable desire to influence events, 'jump the gun'. While *some* of their prescriptions arise from accepted causal connections, others rest on supposition." (Reade, 1974, page 444) Indeed, if Reade were at all interested in the organisation and procedures of planning, then he would base himself on empirical inquiry, and his prescriptions would take the form of applications of the results of such research.

This seems to have a decidedly Popperian ring about it. But, Reade cannot possibly claim that I do not recognise the issue. Thus, in chapter 1 I drew the distinction between a "pattern" and a "deductive" model of explanation, and identified normative theory of planning with the former, at the same time admitting to such shortcomings as it has. Also, as a student of Popper, Reade should know that his methodological and social philosophical work does *not* rest on causal theories either. Here, Popper's reply to Lakatos's worries concerning the falsifiability of the falsificationist principle is relevant (see chapter 1). Far be it from me to put myself in the same league with Popper, but I do claim that we have similar concerns.

Other criticisms by Reade relate to approaches to planning education and need not concern us here. In putting these forward, Reade states as an educational objective to enable students to decide for themselves "... on the basis both of ... cognitive understanding and of ... social philosophical sympathy" what policies to support. If Reade were only to indicate how, he would surely have to invoke rules for deriving statements of policy from statements referring to the facts of the situation and to relevant values. *Rationality*, as advocated in my normative planning theory, *is such a rule*, as we have seen in previous chapters.

I am encouraged in this respect by a further paper by Reade (1985) on "An analysis of the use of the concept of rationality in the literature of planning". In it, Reade challenges me, and others belonging to the category of 'planning writers' which he has singled out for criticism, for using Mannheim's concept of substantive rationality uncritically (see Mannheim, 1940). In particular, he claims we wrongly identify it with Weber's value rationality (see Weber in Gerth and Mills, 1970). I accept this, and the scorn which he pours over me is well deserved.

My position is now, as Reade's is, that there is only *one concept of rationality*. Thus, I reject fundamental distinctions, such as that between functional and substantive rationality used by Mannheim, or between technical and political rationality so fashionable nowadays. With Reade I also agree that "... rational behaviour as generally understood is that which the agent has reason to believe most likely to produce the consequences desired". Nothing more needs to be said about this statement than that it incorporates the demarcation criterion and the rationality rule for decisionmaking which I advocate. I also applaud what Reade says about applying rationality to the choice of goals:

> "There are four ways in which this can be done. First, we can ask whether proposed objectives are in fact attainable; it is not rational to pursue unattainable objectives. Second, we can ask whether, before adopting a given objective, we examined all the possible ones from which we were free to choose; it would not be rational to adopt an objective without doing this, for, having put considerable resources into pursuing it, we might find that we preferred another. Third, we can ask whether our objectives conflict with any higher order objective, or 'end', which we value; it is not rational to engage in activities which infringe our fundamental beliefs. This is so, not only 'logically' but also empirically, in that such infringement can be distressing. Fourth, we can ask the extent to which the various objectives we have in mind are empirically compatible; it is perfectly rational to pursue a multiplicity of competing objectives, since time and other resources are finite, yet all human beings place value on a variety of 'goods'. To deal rationally with this predicament, however, we must attempt to discover *the extent to which* the pursuit of any objective precludes the pursuit of others, and rank the objectives in order of priority." (Reade, 1985, page 79)

But this formulation, which I agree is an improvement upon *Planning Theory*, is very similar to the one used in chapter 6, where I discuss Popper's critical dualism and the role of empirical theories in their technological form. Clearly, Reade and I (both of us drawing on Popper) converge in our understanding of the methodological issues involved in planning to a much greater extent than he might wish to concede. Indeed, his position is so similar to mine that one might describe him as an advocate of rational-comprehensive planning.

9.4 Conclusions

I have learned from Reade more than from most other critics. He has helped in setting me on a course of exploring Popperian philosophy for which I want to thank him.

In particular, the aim of comprehensiveness in *Planning Theory* might be thought to run foul of Popper's strictures against 'holistic' engineering. But we have seen that there can be no objection against attempting comprehensiveness, as long as this is done prudently. Comprehensiveness *must* even be the aim. Otherwise, criticisms could always be rejected by reference to the piecemeal character of planning. The other principles of the "politics of rational planning" can also be shown to be in keeping with the Popperian spirit of criticism: combining various planning agencies to form "multi-planning agencies"; encouraging planners to participate openly in political debates around planmaking; extending this to all planners, and not just the top; aiming for the participation of those concerned. In criticising normative theory of planning, Reade applies criteria which Popper's work does not meet either. In his—rare—pronouncements on how to plan, he reveals a persuasion similar to mine.

Part 3

Conclusions

In this final part, I give a summary of my critical-rationalist planning methodology first. There follows an account of various criticisms of Popper's work. Only one seems of major importance: that directed against consequentialism. Ethical theory teaches us that there are other views of how we should identify correct decisions, but exploring this issue would take us beyond the scope of this work. Rather, we must simply take note of ethical theory forming one of the areas of further research. Others relate to the secondary literature on Popper, in particular that published in German. But above all, other schools of thought in the methodology of science must be analysed for their implications for planning methodology in the same way as this work does with critical rationalism. That would be the most obvious way for advancing planning methodology beyond its present state, which is frankly poorly developed.

A critical-rationalist planning methodology: summary

This chapter provides a summary of the issues in planning methodology and their solutions in the spirit of critical rationalism. It is also argued that, unwittingly, the 'IOR-School', on which my present work draws (see chapter 2), has a philosophy which, when combined with the rationalist outlook of *Planning Theory*, is in tune with critical rationalism. In accord with the structure of the book, in this chapter I will first identify the expectations that we may hold of a critical-rationalist planning methodology, and then give a summary of the argument of Part 2 outlining such a methodology, turning to the 'IOR-School' at the end.

10.1 What to expect of a critical-rationalist planning methodology?

Expectations concerning a critical-rationalist planning methodology must rest on an appreciation of the problems of planning and the nature of methodology.

Planning has many meanings depending on the problem which one wants to tackle. For better or for worse, I have opted for a view of planning as decisionmaking. More in particular, planning stands for efforts to relate our so-called operational decisions (implying definite commitments to action) to each other. This view of planning is identical with that of the Institute for Operational Research. After all, strategic choice stands for exploring the wider implications of decisions. The mainspring of their efforts, and mine, is the quest for rationality, that is for *comprehensively* evaluating possible actions in the light of their consequences. So, they and I wish to broaden the range of consequences which we consider to include the consequences on other decisions with which we are, or may be, confronted, now and in the future.

Methodology is the theory of method. Method relates to the way in which we can, and should, *justify* our arguments. It does *not* dictate how we should *formulate* them. (But it does, of course, suggest methods of work by which we can arrive at acceptable conclusions! The many planning methods which we know are indeed such methods of work.) The emphasis on argument and its justification stems from respect for others. It conceives of our fellow humans as our equals, whom we have a duty to take seriously. In particular, we have to take seriously their *criticisms*. This is the root of the attitude, inherent to methodology, of *rationalism*.

Rationalism, properly conceived, turns upon itself. It recognises that all argument starts from assumptions which, questionable though they may be in themselves, cannot all be questioned at once if we want to avoid being stifled into inaction. In particular, it recognises that there needs to be a fundamental commitment to rationalism, to resolving issues by argument instead of by force. Rationalism which does not recognise these limitations is uncritical, and ultimately self-defeating. *Critical* rationalism recognises that it rests on commitment, and it respects the boundaries of the possible.

Critical-rationalist planning methodology is thus a theory of the method by which we justify our decisions, showing that they are the best available under the current circumstances, that they can be deduced from the definition of the decision-situation. This applies both to operational decisions as well as to decisions involved in adopting plans. It should be noted, once again, that these methods do not dictate how we should *arrive* at plans, only how we should go about *accepting or rejecting* them. It is argued that rationality, as presented in *Planning Theory*, and as implicit in the work of the 'IOR-School', must be conceived as *the* central methodological rule for deciding upon the correctness of decisions, and that consequentialism is the demarcation criterion separating acceptable and unacceptable proposals.

Of course, decisions will seem rational only to those who accept the premises. These form the *definition of the decision-situation*. Many problems in planning—the identification of all alternatives, the weighing of all consequences, including trade-offs between them, the identification and management of uncertainties—have to do with this definition. They are of no consequence for the validity of the consequentialist demarcation criterion, or the rationality rule for that matter.

In the light of this view of planning methodology, the existing planning literature is found wanting where it refers to Popper. As we have seen, a range of works, Braybrooke and Lindblom's classic on *A Strategy of Decision* (1963) in particular, adopt elements of his social philosophy: piecemeal social engineering, negative utilitarianism, and methodological individualism. A more substantial range of books and articles aim at establishing the relevance to planning of his philosophy of science. In arguing that falsification should also be applied to plans, these works fail to recognise the difference between a planning statement expressing, as it does, the intent for action, and universal, or law-like, statements about reality (which is what hypotheses are).

10.2 Fathoming the philosophy of Sir Karl Popper

My criticism of the reception of Popper's work in the existing planning literature has led me to a reassessment of its relevance to planning. I hope that this helps in the search for an intellectually sound approach to environmental planning, which is tolerant and receptive to criticism.

This latter attitude is basic to Popper's philosophy as it emerged during his early years in Vienna, when he was disturbed by the teaching of Marx and Freud and fascinated by the boldness with which Einstein had said that he would recant his theory of relativity if only one crucial experiment would fail to produce the extraordinary result which he had predicted. This example led Popper into the head-on confrontation with logical positivism.

Having delivered his attack in *The Logic of Scientific Discovery* (1959), Popper returned to his concern with the effects of other virulent philosophies of our time, their antecedents and their implications. He did so under the influence of the rise of Nazism from which he had fled, and of Soviet communism. In *The Poverty of Historicism* (1961; first published in 1944/5) and *The Open Society and its Enemies* (1966; 1st edition 1945)—his 'war effort'—he traces these philosophies back to fundamentally wrong assumptions about the nature of knowledge and its relation to action. They make for arrogance as regards the ability to prophesy the future, and for defeatism concerning the way in which the drama of history unfolds. Together, these attitudes account for the spell which these philosophies exercise, making them into powerful weapons in the hands of the enemies of an open—democratic—society. As against this, Popper urges us to accept our responsibility for our fate. In developing this argument, he says much about planning. At the time, central planning seemed one of the distinguishing—and, many thought, superior—features of Nazi Germany and Soviet Russia. Popper shows that central planning is ineffective and leads to the suppression of criticism.

These arguments stick in people's minds when they think about Popper's work. Unthinkingly, they accept a concept of planning that bears the mark of the tense situation of the 1930s and 1940s. My concept of planning is different. It has nothing to do with Popper's "Utopian engineering". Indeed, I am as opposed to centralised blueprint planning as he is. But I can find much in his work which is of even greater relevance for planning methodology than his strictures against blueprint planning.

With these treasures at hand, I set out to develop Popperian planning methodology. Popper's work as such does not provide it. In particular, 'piecemeal engineering'—often held up as a guiding principle—can be shown to be deficient. It merely says what we cannot, and therefore should not, expect of planning. Nor can I agree with those arguing that plans, like hypotheses, should be made falsifiable. Plans are of the nature of singular statements. They can go wrong of course. The application of the Popper-rule to them is nonsensical, nevertheless. The whole force of this rule stems from the fact that hypotheses are *universal* statements. It is only because of this that even a single counterexample, if accepted as genuine, conclusively refutes them. This simply is not true for plans.

Also, the central concern of planning methodology is totally different from that of the methodology of the empirical sciences. I have identified this concern as that of justifying our proposals relating to *decisions*, showing that they are the correct ones to take. Why, then, should the falsificationist principle be applicable, when it is clearly designed only for empirical research?

No, in order to respond to the concerns of planning methodology, we must not introduce standards of justification culled from an entirely different context. We must start from decisions. As regards decisions,

Popper takes a stance which may be described as 'consequentialist': at various occasions, he urges us to consider the consequences of our decisions. Also, he sometimes compares these with the consequences of alternative decisions. Although Popper nowhere draws this conclusion himself, the following seems a fair interpretation of how he would approach decisions. He would consider a proposal concerning a decision as subject to rational assessment if, and only if, it is based on awareness of the expected consequences—intended as well as unintended ones. This is my Popperian demarcation criterion equivalent to falsification for the empirical sciences. Proposals may be considered justified if, and only if, they can be shown to be superior to *all* their alternatives in the light of *all* their consequences. This is the decision rule similar to criteria given by Popper for choosing between different hypotheses (all of them falsifiable, but not yet falsified, that is all of them falling well within the demarcation criterion).

Popper also provides building blocks for the definition of the decision-situation, being the sum of all premises on which the application of the consequentialist demarcation criterion and the rationality rule to specific situations rests. The understanding of any specific situation implies our engaging in *situational analysis* from explicitly defined points of view. Obviously, this is also true for decision-situations.

Defining decision-situations involves both value and factual statements. Neither of these can be derived from the other. This is basic to Popper's *critical dualism*. In it, the application of substantive knowledge in the form of *technological statements* based on empirical laws plays a central part. This is because such technological statements allow us to infer what can *not* be done and/or what consequences (in particular the unintended one's!) we must expect to flow from our actions. All this is compatible with Popper's views on *problemsolving*.

But Popper's consequentialism is nowhere presented as a separate doctrine. Rather, it is derived by way of *reconstruction*: what is *common* to critical dualism, to the doctrine of the application of laws in their technological form and to the law of unintended consequences, is the— unstated—prior assumptions that decisions should be judged by their consequences.

Popper's late philosophy, in particular his evolutionary theory of knowledge and of *World 3*—the world of objective conjectural knowledge, as against World 1 (material objects) and World 2 (subjective experiences)— allows us to interpret the definition of the decision-situation further as a construct of the mind. Although this definition is objective in that it forms part of World 3—and can thus be inspected by others and affect their thoughts and actions—it is subjective at the same time. This is because it always relates to the situation of a subject. This need not be a real subject but can be a construct of our mind, like a nation, the Crown, the public, the community, or 'spaceship earth'. Such constructs are

involved whenever we conceive of decisions being related to each other—
and relating decisions to each other is what planning is about.

This leads into a consideration of the conditions under which a definition
of the decision-situation can be formulated. We cannot conceive of two
people from different cultures, stranded on an island, cooperating
successfully, unless they share at least a modicum of the same language.
In other words, a community of discourse is a *necessary* condition of being
able to arrive at a common definition of a decision-situation. This is even
more true where that definition pertains to an imaginary planning subject.

Beyond this, a *shared meaning* of the concepts involved in defining a
decision-situation forms a *sufficient* condition. If all concepts (including
evaluative ones) are understood to be the same, then there is agreement as
to the definition of the decision-situation, and the decision can be taken.

Even if that situation ever arose, it would be highly unstable.
Planmakers and operational decisionmakers rarely share the meanings of
all their concepts. They occupy different positions in the institutional set-
up. As a result, operational decisionmakers have to reinterpret plans
every time they apply them (often long after they have been made). This
means that they give them their *own* meaning in the light of the concrete
situations which they face. Plans can therefore be merely said to exercise
a form of *plastic control*: they set a context within which operational
decisionmakers find their way, but they do not control them rigidly.

Having formulated the outlines of a planning methodology which I claim
is Popperian in spirit, I looked back on *Planning Theory* and assessed it in
that light. Its emphasis on *comprehensiveness*, although at first sight
seeming to run foul of Popper's strictures against 'holism', is unexceptional
when tempered by the prudence which flows from awareness of human
limitations.

Furthermore, Part 4 of it on "The politics of rational planning"
unwittingly incorporates tenets of Popperian philosophy. Popper would
certainly agree to coordination within multiplanning agencies, and to
engendering more, and more varied, criticism of planning proposals, as
indeed he would to the emphasis on argument instead of force in
implementation; although his theory of intervention would also lead him
to accept that coercion may sometimes be inevitable, in order to prevent
infringments by some upon the freedom of others.

Eric Reade has directed his attention to my concept of theory. He
claims that it is mainly propaganda and not based on empirical research.
But a Popperian would not claim that methodological and ethical
principles, such as Reade's own, should be based solely on empirical
evidence. Popper's work is *not* based on such evidence. Admittedly, the
example of Einstein's theory being tested rigorously triggered off a thought
process in Popper's mind. But that is all that there is to it. It provided
the *occasion* for developing a methodological argument. Its *foundation* lies
elsewhere. It is odd that Reade should overlook this and apply standards

to my work which Popper's work does not meet either. Fortunately,
where he does write about rationality, his views turn out to be very close
to mine.

10.3 The critical rationalism of the 'IOR-School'

In chapter 2, I indicated why, their disclaimer notwithstanding, the 'IOR-
School' adhere to the rationality principle much as I do. This fact
suggests their "strategic choice approach" is also in tune with critical
rationalism. The reason why I raise this question is obvious: I concur
both with this school as well as with Popper. My interest is therefore in
showing that there is no conflict between these two mainsprings of my
present views on planning.

One of the achievements of the 'IOR-School', for which they rightly
enjoy fame, is that of raising our awareness of uncertainty in planning.
Also, this is the reason for their reluctance to talk in terms of rationality,
thinking that this conjures up the idea of certain knowledge. In chapter 2,
I argued that this need not be the case. Here, the point needs to be made
that their whole outlook on knowledge and its application has a distinctly
Popperian ring about it.

This is particularly so where they recognise *various* sources of uncertainty.
That we have imperfect knowledge about the environment is hardly a
revolutionary finding. But they also include uncertainty concerning values.

Indeed, their third form of uncertainty, namely uncertainty concerning
overlapping areas of choice, may be seen as but a variant of uncertainty
about values. It indicates that various actors have different views of their
different, but overlapping, areas of concern.

This reflects the 'agency-centred' view of the 'IOR-School' (see chapter 2).
What is implied in this notion is Popperian situational analysis, described
in chapters 5 and 7. The reader will remember that this is a form of
analysis starting from the point of view of the actor concerned. Decisions
as to the relevance of data can, and must, be taken from that point of
view, lest analysis should deteriorate into collecting a meaningless heap of
facts. It is of little surprise, therefore, to see the 'IOR-School' criticising
surveys, suggesting that they be replaced by deliberate attempts to analyse
decision-situations instead.

Indeed, their strategic choice approach may be given an entirely
Popperian interpretation. It is nothing else but a finely tuned tool for
performing situational analyses. It recommends itself for dealing with
complexity and uncertainty, such as occur in planning. As yet, that is the
only purpose to which it has been put. But I can conceive also of a
historian using strategic choice, bringing situational analysis to perfection
in so doing.

The only remaining difference between the 'IOR-School' and myself is the
importance which I attach to rationality. Here, the distinction between
the 'context of justification' and the 'context of discovery' might help.

In chapter 1, I indicated that rationality as conceived in *Planning Theory* relates only to the context of justification. (Recently, Stewart, 1982, argued similarly without explicit reference to Popper.) If the adherents of the 'IOR-School' could accept that rationality as a methodological rule does not refer so much to the making of decisions, or plans, but to their justification, then we would be in agreement. (This should be possible for them, the more so since, as I could show in the previous chapter, this Popperian distinction runs parallel to theirs between decisiontaking and decisionmaking!) In this way, the danger that they fear, of rationality forming a straightjacket for creativity, would be removed once and for all. Rationality would be a very un-Popperian rule if it had that effect!

10.4 Conclusions
This being a summary statement of a critical-rationalist planning methodology, we now need to consider criticisms which could be levelled against it. Some of them are also levelled against *Planning Theory*. The one which I find most challenging has never been properly formulated. Since it poses a challenge to Popper's (and my) *consequentialism*, it gives me more doubts than the somewhat boring challenges to the idea of rationality in planning in the past. I therefore find it necessary to develop this argument as well as I can, following Popper's example in formulating the doctrine of historicism as well as he could. But I am not at all sure that I can knock this doctrine down, as he has done with historicism.

Possible criticisms

Criticisms of the core of Popper's methodology of science, *falsificationism*, are not relevant to planning methodology. Other criticisms dismiss Popper for his alleged *positivism*. It is not entirely clear whether those who make them mean to condemn Popper's methodology of science as such. They do reject its application to the social sciences and to policymaking. Others castigate Popper's social philosophy for its idealistic view of present Western society.

Lastly, as suggested, criticisms could be directed against Popper's *consequentialism*. Outlining them gives the opportunity of pointing out the relevance of ethical theory to planning methodology.

11.1 Falsificationism
The reader should bear in mind my disclaimer that I would not discuss the merits of Popper's view of science as such. Here, I merely indicate criticisms of it and why I think planning methodologists need not be over-concerned.

A well-known criticism is that made by Kuhn (1962). He shows that scientists do not in fact attempt to falsify their hypotheses. Rather, he portrays scientists as solving puzzles within the confines of pre-established, and relatively stable, paradigms. They are abandoned only when anomalies accumulate. This means oblivion also for those who hold them. Thus, paradigm changes have something of the character of revolutions. Hence the title of Kuhn's book: *The Structure of Scientific Revolutions*.

Lakatos (1978) combines Kuhn's historical interest with Popper's methodological orientation. He argues that falsification is not straight-forward. As we have seen, Popper recognises this but shows that the problem is usually amenable to a pragmatic solution. But Lakatos also argues that a theory should be rejected only if and when a superior alternative is available. Also, like Kuhn, he distinguishes between individual theories and clusters of theories, his "scientific research programmes".

Amongst Popper's former students, Feyerabend (1975) is the most radical of his critics. His argument is directed *Against Method*. Friedmann (1977), in his article discussed in chapter 3, draws his inspiration from him. The argument goes that all methodological rules have been violated in the past by researchers achieving major breakthroughs in so doing. Also, methodology is but a tool in the hands of those in power and is thus suppressive. Feyerabend points to the example of the struggle of established medicine against up-and-coming rivals. Finally, methodology is said to support the claim of science to be a superior way of decisionmaking. It thus inhibits decisionmaking by lay people.

Once again, my purpose is not to discuss these arguments, even less to reject them. I leave the exploration of the implications for planning methodology of these schools of thought in the methodology of science to others. I merely surmise that a planning methodology based on Kuhn or Lakatos, and perhaps even on Feyerabend, may not be all that different from one based on Popper. The validity of consequentialism and the rationality rule does not rest on the validity of falsificationism. Rather, I propose that there is an *analogy* between Popper's arguments and mine, each concerning different problems. Replace the Popper rule by Lakatos's "sophisticated methodological falsificationism", and consequentialism and the rationality rule might still prove valid as a demarcation criterion and as a criterion of choice for decisions. Not all disputes in the methodology of science need have a bearing on planning methodology, therefore.

Clearly, this would be the case with any literal interpretation of Feyerabend rejecting method. But here, too, the case is not clear-cut. His wrath is directed against orthodox applications and misuses of methods. But once his warnings are heeded, and people are able to decide freely whether they want to consult a witchdoctor or an ordinary one, how would they proceed? Would they not assess their chances of being delivered from their illnesses? And would this not be an example of applying rationality?

Maybe my planning methodology is compatible even with logical positivism and its derivatives, schools of thought to which Popper is totally opposed, at least as far as their methodology of the empirical sciences is concerned. The reader will remember that Popper is often identified with logical positivism and the Vienna Circle. He himself denies this and talks about a "Popper-legend" (see Popper's "Replies to my critics", 1974b; in chapter 4 we saw that he even claims to have "killed logical positivism"!). But this concerns problems in the philosophy of the *empirical* sciences: the difference between verificationism and falsificationism as two ways of formulating a "demarcation criterion". Would a critical-rationalist differ from a logical-positivist as regards consequentialism and the rationality rule?

I conjecture that this is not so. True, in its early days, the Vienna Circle dismissed value judgements as meaningless. This would have disturbing consequences for planning, where values play such a crucial role. But according to Kraft, this position quickly changed (Kraft, 1953). Next to Schlick, it was Kraft himself who became concerned prominently with the problem of values. His views do not seem to conflict in any obvious way with my critical-rationalist planning methodology.

Nor do Simon's views developed in his seminal *Administrative Behavior* (1976, 1st edition 1945), his adoption of logical positivism notwithstanding. Clearly, therefore, rooting planning methodology in the philosophy of science would require careful study of more than one school of thought. Perhaps, planning methodologists would then find that they need not get involved in all disputes in this field, simply because there is consensus as regards some of the key issues interesting them.

This brings me back to the starting point of this book as described in the introduction: the need to take cognizance of the methodology of science, and to develop a planning methodology with that awareness in mind. It is to be hoped that this task will fire the imagination of academics in planning much as planning theory attracted attention in the seventies. In particular, a dialogue is needed between the protagonists of various schools of thought in planning methodology.

11.2 Positivism

I mentioned that, his protestations notwithstanding, Popper has often been labelled a positivist during what has come to be called the positivistic dispute in German sociology (Adorno et al, 1976, 1st edition 1969). In view of Popper's opposition to positivism, this is ironic. But during that dispute, the term acquired a different meaning. Whereas, to Popper, positivism is a—misconceived—method which he claims to have refuted conclusively, it is identified nowadays with applying the methods of the natural to the social sciences. Also, in the wake of the positivistic dispute, the term has often been used in a derogatory sense, as if it was identical with everything that was despicable in modern science, from the atomic bomb to opinion polls.

The positivistic dispute has been a decisive influence on the intellectual climate of the seventies. Its effects have been felt somewhat later in Britain and the United States than on the continent of Europe. Nowhere has it failed to affect discussions concerning planning and planning methodology. Often, though, the reception has been superficial.

This cannot be said of Fay (1975). In a work on which the paradigmatic debate in operational research draws (see chapter 2), he distinguishes between three models of the relationship between social theory and political practice: the *positivistic*, the *interpretative*, and the *critical*. I discuss them so as to demonstrate that the charge of positivism is misdirected when applied to critical-rationalist planning methodology.

Fay subsumes Popper under the positivistic model. [A similar fate has befallen me at the hands of Hebbert (1974), and Taylor (1980), arguing that *Planning Theory* has a positivistic ring about it.] Yet the meaning of this model is not at all clear. Fay says that it does *not* refer to

"... a process of analysis by which various consequences of particular courses of action are spelled out in terms of their monetary cost and benefit so that a decision-maker may be well informed as to the possible outcomes of his alternatives. A policy science in this sense is intended ... to 'map the decision space' in which the policy-maker is going to act." (1975, page 14)

Note that, if only the unfortunate limitation to monetary costs and benefits was dropped (this being an odd statement for somebody like Fay), this would be a view of decisionmaking and planning identical to mine.

But what, then, *is* the positivistic view? Its distinguishing feature, according to Fay, is that the best course of action is identified *by the policy analyst.* He therefore becomes what Fay labels a social—or policy—engineer. (Habermas would describe this view of policy science as technocratic; see Habermas, 1968.)

Now, this clearly is *not* the view which either Popper or I hold.

But some other criticisms which Fay levels against Popper may still apply, such as the charge of ideologically supporting industrial society. Thomas (1979) has said as much with respect to me.

Fay's second model, the interpretative one,

"... starts with the fact that a large part of the vocabulary of social science is comprised of *action concepts* ..." (page 71).

This is, of course, also true for my planning methodology. Nor am I (or would, for that matter, Popper!) be impressed by Fay claiming that explanations of actions are contextual, and ultimately rooted in social practices and underlying constitutive meanings. I refer the reader to chapters 2, 7, and 8.

Fay further characterises interpretative social science as

"... one which reveals to people what it is that they and others are doing when they act and speak as they do. It does this by articulating the symbolic structures in accordance with which people in a particular social setting act. By making clear the criteria of rationality in virtue of which certain alternatives were chosen rather than others, ... an interpretative social science uncovers the connections which exist between parts of people's lives, thereby allowing one to see these lives in the whole ... The result of this sort of analysis is thus a kind of enlightenment ..." (page 81).

With some imagination, this could be regarded as describing what happens in strategic choice, being an operational version of my decision-centred view. Its originators even claim that the "invisible product" of planning, in terms of greater awareness on the part of those involved, is more important than the resulting plans, strategies, and the like (see Carter et al., 1975, page 20).

A few pages further down, Fay summarises this model by saying that the

"... aim of an interpretative social theory is to make possible a successful dialogue in speaking and acting between different social actors or within oneself." (pages 81-82)

He adds this footnote:

"One result of this would be to foster a tolerance and respect for others which is an essential prerequisite for a democratic social order; moreover, it would presumably lessen the attractiveness of violence as a way of dealing with those with whom one disagrees."

Again, this is what Popper says, as we have seen in chapters 1 and 4.
I can again but conclude that the views developed in this work nowhere
conflict with Fay's interpretative model and that it must, therefore, escape the
verdict of positivism. Fay's third model though leads us to an exploration
of yet another criticism of Popper's work (and mine).

11.3 Idealism

Fay's interpretative model is similar to what I propose in the wake of Popper
(the positivistic model being a straw man and not a serious proposition).
This makes his criticisms of the interpretative model particularly interesting.
He enunciates four which cumulatively lead to the adoption of the critical
model: that it gives no room for an examination of the conditions which
give rise to action; that it neglects the unintended consequences of action;
that it does not understand conflict; that it cannot offer an explanation of
historical change. Such charges are summarised by saying that the views
concerned are *idealist*, that is, laying too much store by deliberate action
and paying too little attention too structural determinants.

Although accepting the necessity of interpretative categories in the social
sciences, proponents of the critical model insist

> "... that a great many of the actions people perform are caused by social
> conditions over which they have no control, and that a great deal of
> what people do to one another is not the result of conscious knowledge
> and choice ..." (Fay, 1975, page 94).

Would Popper deny this? He has been shown in chapter 7 to draw
attention to the 'law of unintended consequences' himself. The main
purpose, according to him, of the social sciences is just to explore these
consequences, caused, as they often are, by the working of social institutions.

So, if the charge of idealism does not relate to whether Popper recognises
in principle that social conditions influence people's actions, what then
does it amount to? I think it comes down to different judgements as to
the scope for deliberate change. It is indeed possible to disagree with
Popper concerning Western societies and whether it is worthwhile to aim
for improvements within that context. Thus, one could say that Popper's
assessment of the chances of rational argument prevailing is idealistic.
Cornforth (1968), in his book-size reply to *The Open Society and its Enemies*
challenges Popper on precisely this point:

> "... one may ask, is a society really 'open' when social production is tied
> to ensuring the accumulation of capital from surplus value, and the
> enjoyment of benefits and privileges by some depends on exploiting the
> labour of others? And can one's mind be really 'open' so long as one
> is unable to see that such is the case with contemporary capitalist society,
> or to see the possibilities of advance which could be opened up for mankind
> if only the exploitation of men by men were done away with?" (page 6)

As I said, this point is legitimate. It has also been raised against *Planning Theory* by Friedmann (1974), Cooke and Reese (1977), Scott and Roweis (1977), and Thomas (1979). But we should be clear as to what the issue is. It is not one of the *methodology* of planning but concerns a matter of substance: the state of the society in which we live. Whether we condemn it or hold it up as a model for the rest of the world (as Popper sometimes does) need not interfere with our judgements concerning how decisions should be taken.

In the context of this book, therefore, I decline to discuss whether it is idealistic to propose a critical-rationalist planning methodology. Clearly, critics have in mind barriers to rational choice; which they claim exist in present society. The onus is on them to demonstrate that, if these were removed, planning would be *different* from the way I see it, that different methodological rules would hold, implying different methods of work. Meanwhile, I draw courage from such evidence as there is of planning in Socialist countries using methods which are suspiciously like those of Western planning.

11.4 Consequentialism
What may be problematic for my Popperian planning methodology are arguments in ethical theory against consequentialism.

I can do no more than explore this issue, drawing on Frankena (1973, 1st edition 1963) presenting a "theory of obligation" designed to guide us in the making of decisions "... about actions in particular situations ..." (page 12). He distinguishes teleological and deontological theories:

"A teleological theory says that the basis or ultimate criterion or standard of what is morally right ... is the ... comparative balance of good over evil produced. Thus, an act is *right* if and only if it or the rule under which it falls produces, will probably produce, or is intended to produce *at least as great a balance of good over evil* as any available alternative ..." (page 14).

Evidently, this is the consequentialist ethics of Popper and myself. More in particular, it includes both the consequentialist demarcation criterion as well as the rationality rule for choosing between alternatives.

The best known teleological theories are utilitarian, involving variants of Bentham's "felicific calculus": the greatest happiness for the greatest number. As against this, deontologists assert that

"... there are other considerations that may make an action or rule right or obligatory besides the goodness or badness of its consequences— certain features of the act itself other than the *value* it brings into existence, for example, the fact that it keeps a promise, is just, or is commanded by God or by the state." (page 15)

Frankena's objection to teleological theories, in particular to utilitarianism, is that they are unable to deal with issues of justice:

> "... an action, practice, or rule may maximize the sum of good in the world, and yet be unjust in the way in which it distributes this sum, so that a less beneficient one that is more just may be preferable." (page 41)

His own theory of obligation is mixed. It is a deontological one, but closer to teleological, and in particular to utilitarian theories than many others. It insists

> "... that we are to determine what is right or wrong in particular situations, normally at least, by consulting rules such as we usually associate with morality, but ... the way to tell what rules to live by is to see which rules best fulfil the joint requirements of utility and justice ..." (page 44).

Thus, one should try to achieve nonmoral goods, but their pursuit must be tempered by considerations of justice.

By justice, Frankena means *distributive* justice. He opts for equality as its basic standard, but he admits considerations of needs in determining the actual distribution of goods.

Considerations of distributive justice are not exactly alien to environmental planners. They have even gained some prominence during recent years as a result of the realisation of the uneven distributional effects of many planning proposals. Kiernan (1982) is but one example of authors advocating positive discrimination:

> "The principle might require, as a condition of a development approval, that a certain proportion of the construction jobs associated with a project be made available to special needs groups who would otherwise be excluded. It might insist that a seemingly disproportionate number of public recreation facilities and programs be located in a given low-income area in order to compensate for the absence of private recreational opportunities. It might require assurance of the availability of alternative low-cost accommodation before permits were issued for the demolition of existing low-income housing ...

> "Nor need this principle be restricted to the *substantive* side of the planning dialectic; it could and should be practised with respect to *process* as well. In fact, it may be even more important for planners to build the principle of positive discrimination into such planning processes as citizen participation and environmental and social impact analysis ... If we were to ... structure these and other planning processes to articulate and emphasise the concerns of the disadvantaged as a first priority, we could move beyond equality of opportunity to equality of results." (page 22)

The argument is hardly as revolutionary as Kiernan makes it to be. But the key question that interests us here is whether it involves a different theory of ethics, or whether discrimination in favour of the disadvantaged could not be justified on consequentialist grounds. It is identical to that raised by Attfield (1983) concerning *The Ethics of Environmental Concern*. Against the widely held belief that the environmental crisis requires a new ethics, he contends that "... there already exist the moral resources to challenge and condemn the malpractices which lead to the despoilation of nature" (page 194). These existing approaches—above all, consequentialism—can be suitably adapted.

A wider interpretation of consequentialist ethics might indeed *include* distributional, alongside other effects of actions. Equally, it might encompass the interests of future generations, this being one of the issues which concern environmentalists. Neither Popper's nor my interpretation of rationality would exclude this.

In this respect, I draw courage from Singer (1979) coming down on the side of a broadly utilitarian interpretation of ethics. He derives this from the *universal view* which he argues is inherent to ethics:

"This does not mean that a particular ethical judgment must always be universally applicable. Circumstances alter cases, as we have seen. What it does mean is that in making ethical judgments we go beyond our likes and dislikes ... Ethics requires us to go beyond 'I' and 'you' to the universal law, the universalizable judgment, the standpoint of the impartial spectator or ideal observer, or whatever we choose to call it ..." (page 11).

Many ethical theories fit these criteria. But it is difficult to find a common denominator. Singer suggests cautiously though that the "... universal aspect of ethics ... does provide a persuasive, although not conclusive, reason for taking a broadly utilitarian position." (page 12)

"My reason for suggesting this is as follows. In accepting that ethical judgments must be made from a universal point of view, I am accepting that my own interests cannot, simply because they are *my* interests, count more than the interests of anyone else. Thus my very natural concern that my own interests be looked after must ... be extended to the interests of others ...

"In place of my own interests, I now have to take account of the interests of all those affected by my decision. This requires me to weigh up all these interests and adopt the course of action most likely to maximise the interests of those affected. Thus I must choose the course of action which has the best consequences, on balance, for all affected. This is a form of utilitarianism. It differs from classical utilitarianism in that 'best consequences' is understood as meaning what, on balance, furthers the interests of those affected, rather than merely what increases pleasure and reduces pain." (pages 12-13)

This shows utilitarianism (consequentialism, as indicated, according to Regan, 1980) to be deducible from the universal aspects of ethics, but Singer agrees that there are other ethical ideals which are universal yet incompatible with some versions of utilitarianism:

"It does show that we very swiftly arrive at an *initially* utilitarian position ... This ... places the onus of proof on those who seek to go beyond utilitarianism. The utilitarian position is a minimal one, a first base which we reach by universalizing self-interested decisionmaking." (page 13)

Singer's book confirms the relevance of ethics to planning methodology, pointed out by Taylor (1980) in his paper discussed in chapter 3. It also indicates its limits. Planning, being concerned with rational action, need *not* be ethically motivated. It can simply be self-regarding. A condition of planning being not only rational, but also ethically sound is what Singer terms conscientiousness:

"People who are conscientious will, if they accept the values of their society ... always tend to promote what the society values ... Moreover, those motivated by the desire to do what is right can be relied upon to act as they think right in all circumstances ... Conscientiousness is thus a kind of multi-purpose gap-filler that can be used to motivate people towards whatever is valued ...

"On this view of ethics it is still results, not motives, that really matter. Conscientiousness is of value because of its consequences. Yet, unlike, say, benevolence, conscientiousness can be ... encouraged for its own sake." (page 210)

Therefore, for planning to be not only methodologically but also ethically acceptable, my present concern for rules may have to be expanded to include the way definitions of decision-situations are arrived at, whether this is done conscientiously. Like Attfield (1983) accepting the (consequentialist) cost-benefit analysis but criticising, amongst others, "the lust for short-term returns" (page 194) as evidenced by the way in which future costs and benefits are discounted, this means attending to metaphysical views underlying definitions of decision situations, whilst at the same time accepting a rationalist methodology of decisionmaking and planning.

My aim was to demonstrate the relevance of ethical theory to planning. (On the same topic see also Kaufman, 1981; Wachs, 1985.) It is beyond me to give decisive reasons for preferring consequentialism—the "broadly utilitarian position" which Singer defends. Deontology is a potential challenge, therefore, to the Popperian planning methodology which I put foreward in this book.

11.5 A note on further work in the methodology of planning

The theory of ethics is not the only area in which more work could be done. Closely related to ethics is what has come to be known as the "theory of action" (for example, see Davis, 1979). But what comes to mind even more directly is an expansion of the present analysis to include the secondary literature.

The German literature deserves particular attention. For reasons of his critique of Marxism, Popper is being adopted as a philosopher by political groups from the conservative right to the non-Marxist social-democratic left. Similar inclinations exist in Britain, such as Magee (1973) claiming Popper's philosophy to be essentially social-democratic, and James (1980) drawing support from Popper's writings for a position which one can describe as enlightened conservatism, this apart from Sir Edward Boyle embracing Popper (see Boyle, 1974). But, as yet, no British Prime Minister is known to have written a philosophical foreword to a reader on critical rationalism and social democracy, such as the former Federal Chancellor Helmut Schmidt has done (see Lührs et al, 1975).

So much for the prominence which Popper's philosophy has gained in Germany. This drafting of Popper into party politics has evoked criticism, and not from Marxists alone. In a whole series of books, Spinner (1974; 1977; 1978) castigates the "new critical rationalism" and claims to advocate a more radical pluralism than Popper. Also, he attempts to protect Popper's philosophy against his "friends". In so doing, he also does not hesitate to criticise Popper savagely. His tone is sometimes reminiscent of Feyerabend's tirades against his former teacher, although Spinner (1978, pages 210 and 586-591) has serious misgivings about Feyerabend, too. (Feyerabend ridicules him for that; see Feyerabend, 1980, pages 202-207.)

Any study of the reception of critical rationalism in the German literature would have to attend also to the extensive work of Albert (see, in particular, 1969, 1st edition 1968; 1978). The latter is well known, even to English-speaking readers, for his role as main protagonist on the side of the critical rationalists in the positivistic dispute. Albert is more interested than Popper in the application of critical rationalism to decisionmaking. Clearly, this makes a study of his work particularly useful for our purposes.

Subsequent work might also concern philosophical assumptions underlying critical rationalism, but this would lead us further away from planning methodology. One such assumption is that of the existence of reality, another that of a free will. It takes only a few moments' reflection to understand that such assumptions have a bearing on planning.

Nor should this surprise us. Planning is an intensely human activity. It brings out the best in us in terms of consciously guiding our actions, but it can also bring out the worst when our actions aim at harming others. Some clear thinking about the issues involved seems to be in order. Philosophical inquiry may contribute to this end.

References

Ackoff R L, 1979a, "The future of operational research is past" *Journal of the Operational Research Society* **30** 93–104

Ackoff R L, 1979b, "Resurrecting the future of operational research" *Journal of the Operational Research Society* **30** 189–199

Ackoff R L, Emery F E, 1972 *On Purposeful Systems* (Atherton, Chicago)

Adorno Th W, Dahrendorf R, Pilot H, Albert H, Habermas J, Popper K R, 1976 *The Positivistic Dispute in German Sociology* (Heinemann, London) (German edition published 1969 under *Der Positivismusstreit in der deutschen Soziologie* by Luchterhand, Neuwied)

Albert H, 1969 *Traktat über kritische Vernunft* 1st edition, 1968 [J C B Mohr (Paul Siebeck), Tübingen]

Albert H, 1978 *Traktat über rationale Praxis* [J C B Mohr (Paul Siebeck), Tübingen]

Archibald K A, 1980, "The pitfalls of language, or analysis through the looking-glass", in *Pitfalls of Analysis*, Eds G Majone, E S Quade (John Wiley, New York) 179–199

Attfield R, 1983 *The Ethics of Environmental Concern* (Basil Blackwell, Oxford)

Barnard C I, 1938 *The Functions of the Executive* (Harvard University Press, Cambridge, MA)

Batty M, 1980, "Limits to prediction in science and design" *Design Studies*, **1** 153–159

Boardman P, 1978 *The Worlds of Patrick Geddes—Biologist, Town Planner, Re-educator, Peace-warrior* (Routledge and Kegan Paul, Henley-on-Thames,Oxon)

Boyle E, 1974, "Karl Popper's *Open Society*: A personal appreciation" in *The Philosophy of Karl Popper, Volume 2* Ed. P A Schilpp (Open Court, La Salle, IL) pp 843–858

Braybrooke D, Lindblom C E, 1963, *A Strategy of Decision—Policy Evaluation as a Social Process* (The Free Press, New York)

Breheny M J, Hooper A J (Eds), 1985 *Rationality in Planning. Critical Essays on the Role of Rationality in Urban and Regional Planning* (Pion, London)

Bussink F L, 1980 *Plannen voor stadsvernieuwing* (Samsom, Alphen aan den Rijn)

Camhis M, 1979 *Planning Theory and Philosophy* (Tavistock, London)

Cammen H van der, 1979 *De binnenkant van de planologie* (Coutinho, Muiderberg)

Carter K R, Friend J K, Pollard J de B, Yewlett C J L, 1975 *Organisational Influences in the Regional Strategy Process* (Institute for Operational Research/ Department of Urban and Regional Planning, Lanchester Polytechnic, Coventry, England)

Chadwick G A, 1978 *A Systems View of Planning* 1st edition, 1970 (Pergamon Press, Oxford)

Cooke P, Reese G, 1977, "Faludi's 'Sociology in planning education': A critical comment" *Urban Studies* **14** 219–222

Cornforth M, 1968 *The Open Philosophy and the Open Society* (Lawrence and Wishart, London)

Dando M R, Bennett P G, 1981, "A Kuhnian crisis in management science?" *Journal of the Operational Research Society* **32** 91–103

Davis L H, 1979 *Theory of Action* (Prentice Hall, Englewood Cliffs, NJ)

Donnison D, 1972, "Ideologies and policies", *Journal of Social Policy* **1** 97–117

Drake M, McLoughlin J B, Thompson R, Thornley J, 1975, "Aspects of structure planning in Britain", RP-20 (Centre for Environmental Studies, London)

Dunn E S, 1971 *Economic and Social Development* (The Johns Hopkins University Press, Baltimore, MD)

Etzioni A, 1968 *The Active Society* (The Free Press, New York)

Eversley D, 1973 *The Planner in Society* (Faber and Faber, London)

Faludi A (Ed.), 1973 *A Reader in Planning Theory* (Pergamon Press, Oxford)

Faludi A, 1982, "Three paradigms of planning theory", in *Planning Theory—Prospects for the 1980s* Eds P Healey, G McDougall, M Thomas (Pergamon Press, Oxford) pp 81-101

Faludi A, 1983, "Critical rationalism and planning methodology" *Urban studies* **20** 265-278

Faludi A, 1984 *Planning Theory* first published, 1973 (Pergamon Press, Oxford)

Faludi A, 1985, "The return of rationality", in *Rationality in Planning. Critical Essays on the Role of Rationality in Urban and Regional Planning* Eds M J Breheny, A J Hooper (Pion, London) pp 27-47

Faludi A, Mastop J M, 1982, "The 'IOR-School': the development of a planning methodology", *Environment and Planning B* **9** 241-256

Fay B, 1975 *Social Theory and Political Practice* (George Allen and Unwin, Hemel Hempstead, Herts)

Feyerabend P, 1975 *Against Method—Outlines of an Anarchistic Theory of Knowledge* (New Left Books, London)

Feyerabend P, 1980 *Erkenntnis für freie Menschen* (Suhrkamp, Frankfurt am Main)

Frankena W K, 1973 *Ethics* 1st edition, 1963 (Prentice-Hall, Englewood Cliffs, NJ)

Frazer J W, Boland L A, 1983, "An essay on the foundation of Friedman's methodology" *American Economic Review* **73** 129-144

Freeman M, 1975, "Sociology and Utopia: some reflections on the social philosophy of Karl Popper" *British Journal of Sociology* **26** 20-34

Friedmann J, 1966/67, "Planning as a vocation" *Plan CANADA* **6** 99-124; **7** 8-25

Friedmann J, 1967, "A conceptual model for the analysis of planning behavior" *Administrative Science Quarterly* **12** 225-252; see also: Faludi A (Ed.), 1973, *A Reader in Planning Theory* (Pergamon Press, Oxford) pp 345-370

Friedmann J, 1973 *Retracking America* (Doubleday, New York)

Friedmann J, 1974, "Planning Theory—Review" *Regional Studies* **8** 311

Friedmann J, 1977, "The epistemology of social practice" *Theory and Society* **6** 75-92

Friend J K, Jessop W N, 1977 *Local Government and Strategic Choice* 1st edition, published by Tavistock, London, in 1969) (Pergamon Press, Oxford)

Friend J K, Power J M, Yewlett C J L, 1974 *Public Planning—The Inter-corporate Dimension* (Tavistock, London)

Gendin A M, 1969, "Societal prognosis and Popper's interpretation" *Soviet Studies in Philosophy* **8** 148-168

Gerth H H, Mills C W, 1970 *From Max Weber* (Routledge and Kegan Paul, Henley-on-Thames, Oxon)

Gillingwater D, 1975 *Regional Planning and Social Change* (Saxon House, Farnborough, Hants)

Gould J, 1971 *The Rational Society* Auguste Comte Memorial Lecture (The Athlone Press, London)

Gray G, 1976, "The liberalism of Karl Popper" *Government and Opposition* **11** 337-355

Gunsteren H R van, 1976 *The Quest for Control—A Critique of the Rational-Central-Rule Approach in Public Affairs* (John Wiley, Chichester, Hants)

Habermas J, 1968, "Techniek und Wissenschaft als Ideologie" in *Techniek und Wissenschaft als Ideologie* (Suhrkamp, Frankfurt) pp 48-103

Harris B, 1978, "A note on planning theory", *Environment and Planning A* **10** 221-224

Hart D A, 1973, "Ordering change and changing order" *Policy and Politics* **2** 1-21

Hart D A, 1976 *Strategic Planning in London—The Rise and Fall of the Primary Road Network* (Pergamon Press, Oxford)

Harvey D W, 1973, *Social Justice and the City* (Edward Arnold, London)

Hayek F A, 1960, "Housing and town planning" in *The Constitution of Liberty* (Routledge and Kegan Paul, Henley-on-Thames, Oxon) pp 340–357

Hayek F A, 1962 *The Road to Serfdom* 1st edition, 1944 (Routledge and Kegan Paul, Henley-on-Thames, Oxon)

Hebbert M, 1974, "Planning Theory—Review" *Planning Outlook* **17** 43–47

Heywood P, 1982, "Creativity and control in the environmental design professions" *Planscape* **1** 3–12

Hickling A, 1974 *Managing Decisions* (Mantec, Rugby, Warwicks)

Hickling A, 1975 *Aids to Strategic Choice* Centre for Continuing Education, University of British Columbia, Vancouver

Hooper A, 1982, "Methodological monism or critical dualism? Reflections on Andreas Faludi's Planning Theory", *Built Environment* **8** 247–248.

James R, 1980 *Return to Reason—Popper's Thought in Public Life* (Open Books, Shepton Mallet, Somerset)

Kaplan A, 1964 *The Conduct of Inquiry—Methodology for Behavioral Science* (Harper and Row, New York)

Kaufman J L, 1981, "Teaching planning ethics" *Journal of Planning Education and Research* **1** 29–35

Kiernan M, 1982, "Ideology and the precarious future of the Canadian planning profession" *Plan CANADA* **22** 14–24

Koertge N, 1979, "The methodological status of Popper's rationality principle" *Theory and Decision* **10** 83–95

Kraft V, 1953, *The Vienna Circle* (Greenwood Press, New York)

Kreukels A M J, 1980 *Planning and Planning Process* (VUGA, The Hague)

Kreukels A M J, 1982, "The planning debate in The Netherlands: Implications of the four background reports of the W.R.R. Preliminary Studies Series on approaches to planning" *Planning and Development in The Netherlands* **14** 3–32

Kuhn T S, 1962, *The Structure of Scientific Revolutions* (Chicago University Press, Chicago, IL)

Lakatos I, 1978 *The Methodology of Scientific Research Programmes, Philosophical Papers Volume 1* (Cambridge University Press, Cambridge)

Leach S, 1982, "In defence of the rational model" in *Approaches in Public Policy* Eds S Leach, J Stewart (George Allen and Unwin, Hemel Hempstead, Herts)

Lindblom C E, 1965, *The Intelligence of Democracy—Decision Making Through Mutual Adjustment* (The Free Press, New York)

Lippmann W, 1937, *The Good Society* (Little, Brown, Boston, MA)

Los M, 1981, "Some reflexions on epistemology, design and planning" in *Urbanization and Urban Planning in Capitalist Society* Eds M Dear, A J Scott (Methuen, London) pp 63–88

Lührs G, Sarrazin Th, Spreer F, Tietzel M, 1975 *Kritischer Rationalismus und Sozialdemokratie I* (J H W Dietz Nachf., Berlin)

Magee B, 1973, *Popper* (Fontana/Collins, London)

Majone G, 1980, "Policies as theories" *Omega* **8** 151–162

Mannheim K, 1940 *Man and Society in an Age of Reconstruction* (Kegan Paul, London)

McConnell S, 1981 *Theories for Planning—An Introduction* (Heinemann, London)

Medawar P, 1974, "Hypothesis and imagination" in *The Philosophy of Karl Popper, Volume 1* Ed. P A Schilpp (Open Court, La Salle, IL) pp 274–291

Meyerson M, Banfield E C, 1955 *Politics, Planning and the Public Interest—The Case of Public Housing in Chicago* (The Free Press, Glencoe, IL)

Moewes W, 1980 *Grundfragen der Lebensraumgestaltung* (De Gruyter, Berlin)

Mussachia M M, 1977, "Some comments on scientific historical predictability and Karl Popper's refutation of its possibility" *International Studies in Philosophy* **9** 85–92.

Needham B, 1971, "Planning as problem-solving" *Journal of the Royal Town Planning Institute* **57** 317–319

Needham B, 1977 *How Cities Work* (Pergamon Press, Oxford)

Needham B, 1982 *Choosing the Right Policy Instruments* (Gower, Aldershot, Hants)

Needham B, Faludi A, 1973, "Planning and the public interest" *Journal of the Royal Town Planning Institute* **59** 164–166

Parekh B, 1982 *Contemporary Political Thinkers* (Martin Robertson, Oxford)

Passmore J, 1975, "The Poverty of Historicism revisited" *Historische Theorie* **14** (supplement) 30–47

Perloff H S, with the assistance of Friedmann J R P, 1957, "Education and research in planning: A Review of the University of Chicago Experiment" in *Education for Planning—City, State and Regional* H S Perloff (The Johns Hopkins University Press, Baltimore, MD) pp 133–167

Popper K R, 1935 *Logik der Forschung* (Julius Springer, Vienna)

Popper K R, 1959 *The Logic of Scientific Discovery* (Hutchinson, London)

Popper K R, 1961 *The Poverty of Historicism* first published in 1944/5 (Routledge and Kegan Paul, Henley-on-Thames, Oxon)

Popper K R, 1963 *Conjectures and Refutations* (Routledge and Kegan Paul, Henley-on-Thames, Oxon)

Popper K R, 1966 *The Open Society and its Enemies* 2 volumes, 1st edition 1945 (Routledge and Kegan Paul, Henley-on-Thames, Oxon)

Popper K R, 1973 *Objective Knowledge* 1st edition 1972 (Oxford University Press, Oxford)

Popper K R, 1974a, "Autobiography of Karl Popper" in *The Philosophy of Karl Popper, Volume* 1 Ed. P A Schilpp (Open Court, La Salle, IL) pp 1–184

Popper K R, 1974b, "Replies to my critics" in *The Philosophy of Karl Popper, Volume* 1 Ed. P A Schilpp (Open Court, La Salle, IL) pp 961–1197

Popper K R, Eccles J C, 1977 *The Self and its Brain* (Springer, New York)

Rawls J, 1971 *A Theory of Justice* (Oxford University Press, Oxford)

Reade E J, 1974, 'Review of 'Planning Theory'" *The Town Planning Review* **45** 444–446

Reade E J, 1976, "The context of 'theory' courses in town planning education" in WP-25, Department of Town Planning, Oxford Polytechnic pp 94–136

Reade E J, 1983, "Monitoring in planning" in *Evaluating Urban Planning Efforts,* Ed. I Masser (Gower, Aldershot, Hants) pp 224–242

Reade E J, 1985, "An analysis of the use of the concept of rationality in the literature of planning" in *Rationality in Planning: Critical Essays on the Role of Rationality in Urban and Regional Planning* Eds M J Breheny, A J Hooper (Pion, London) pp 77–97

Regan D, 1980 *Utilitarianism and Co-operation* (Clarendon Press, Oxford)

Rittel H J W, Webber M M, 1973, "Dilemmas of a general theory of planning" *Policy Sciences* **4** 155–169

Rosenhead J, 1980a, "Planning under uncertainty: 1 The inflexibility of methodologies" *Journal of the Operational Research Society* **31** 209–216

Rosenhead J, 1980b, "Planning under uncertainty: 2 A methodology for robustness analysis" *Journal of the Operational Research Society* **31** 331–341.

Schilpp P A (Ed.), 1974 *The Philosophy of Karl Popper* 2 volumes (The Open Court, La Salle, IL)

Scott A J, Roweis S T, 1977, "Urban planning theory and practice: A reappraisal" *Environment and Planning A* **9** 1097–1119

Settle T, 1974, "Induction and probability unfused" in *The Philosophy of Karl Popper* Ed. P A Schilpp (The Open Court, La Salle, IL) 697–749

Shaw P D, 1971, "Popper, historicism, and the remaking of society" *Philosophy of the Social Sciences* **1** 299–308

Simon H A, 1976 *Administrative Behavior* 1st edition, 1945 (The Free Press, New York)

Singer P, 1979 *Practical Ethics* (Cambridge University Press, Cambridge)

Spinner H F, 1974 *Pluralismus als Erkenntnismodel* (Suhrkamp, Frankfurt am Main)

Spinner H F, 1977 *Begründung, Rationalität und Kritik—Zur philosophischen Grundlagenproblematik des Rechtfertigungsmodells der Erkenntnis und der kritizistischen Alternative—Band 1: Die Entstehung des Erkenntnisproblems im griechischen Denken und seine klassische Rechtfertigungslösung aus dem Geist des Rechts* (Vieweg, Braunschweig)

Spinner H F, 1978 *Popper und die Politik—I. Geschlossenheitsprobleme* (J H W Dietz Nachf., Berlin)

Spreer F, 1974 *Zur Wissenschaftstheorie der Wirtschaftsplanung* (Neue Gesellschaft, Bonn–Bad Godesberg)

Stewart J, 1982, "Guidelines for policy derivation" in *Approaches in Public Policy* Eds S Leach, J Stewart (George Allen and Unwin, London)

Suchting W A, 1972, "Marx, Popper, and 'historicism'" *Inquiry* **15** 235–266

Sutton A, Hickling A, Friend J K, 1977, "The analysis of policy options in structure plan preparation" IP—IOR/932 (Institute for Operational Research, Coventry)

Taylor N, 1980, "Planning theory and the philosophy of planning" *Urban Studies* **17** 159–172

Thomas H D, Minett J M, Hopkins S, Hamnett S L, Faludi A, Barrell D, 1983 *Flexibility and Commitment in Planning—A Comparative Study of Local Planning and Development in The Netherlands and England* (Martinus Nijhoff, The Hague)

Thomas M J, 1979, "The procedural planning theory of A. Faludi" *Planning Outlook* **22** 72–76; also included in *Critical Readings in Planning Theory* Ed. C Paris, 1982, (Pergamon Press, Oxford) pp 13–25

Urbach P, 1978, "Is any of Popper's arguments against historicism valid?" *British Journal of Philosophy* **24** 117–130

Wachs M (Ed.), 1985 *Ethics in Planning* (The Centre for Urban Policy Research, The State University of New Jersey, New Brunswick, NJ)

Wilson A G, 1969, "The use of analogies in geography and planning" WP-32 (Centre for Environmental Studies, London)

For obvious reasons, the name of Karl Popper has not been indexed. On the other hand, his major works have been under their titles *Autobiography*, (*The*) *Logic of Scientific Discovery*, (*The*) *Open Society and its Enemies*, (*The*) *Poverty of Historicism*, (*The*) *Self and its Brain*. Also included in the index is *Planning Theory* by the author.